The Autobiography of a Winnebago Indian

D0360519

by
Paul Radin

DOVER PUBLICATIONS, INC.
NEW YORK

Published in Canada by General Publishing Company, Ltd., 30 Lesmill Road, Don Mills, Toronto, Ontario.

Published in the United Kingdom by Constable and Company, Ltd., 10 Orange Street, London W. C. 2.

This new Dover edition, first published in 1963, is an unabridged and unaltered republication of the work first published by the University of California Press in the *University of California Publications in American Archaeology and Ethnology*, Volume 16, No. 7, April 15, 1920.

The publisher is grateful to the Library of Columbia University for making a copy of this book available for reproduction purposes.

Standard Book Number: 486-20096-5

Library of Congress Catalog Card Number: 63-17914

Manufactured in the United States of America
Dover Publications, Inc.
180 Varick Street
New York, N. Y. 10014

INTRODUCTION

One of the greatest drawbacks in the study of primitive peoples is the difficulty, one might almost say the impossibility, of obtaining an inside view of their culture from their own lips and by their own initiative. A native informant is, at best, interested merely in satisfying the demands of the investigator. The limitations thus imposed as regards the nature and extent of the knowledge furnished are further increased by the circumstances under which the knowledge is usually imparted, circumstances of a nature tending to destroy practically all the subjective values associated with the particular ritual, myth, or what not, that is being narrated.

Many of these defects could possibly be obviated if the investigator became a member of the tribe, but this is generally out of the question. It would mean spending a good portion of one's life in a primitive community, and that no well-qualified ethnologist is prepared to do, even were funds available for the purpose. As a result individuals but partially qualified to describe accurately the life of a primitive community—for example, missionaries, soldiers, and ethnological adventurers—are the only ones who ever spend large portions of their lives among aboriginal tribes. Even when such investigators are conscientious and strive to be open-minded and fair, it is only on rare occasions that they succeed in presenting the facts in an emotional setting, and when they do make such an attempt, the result is generally so completely tinged with the investigator's own emotional tone as to be quite unsafe to follow.

For a long time most ethnologists have realized that the lack of "atmosphere" in their descriptions is a very serious and fundamental defect, and that this defect could only be properly remedied by having a native himself give an account of his particular culture. Unfortunately, however, natives never spend much time trying to get a general idea of their culture and are consequently unable to describe it when pressed. The only possibility of obtaining any direct expression has therefore to be sought in another way. Unprepared as primitive man is to give a well-rounded and complete account of his culture, he has always been willing to narrate snatches of autobiography. Such personal reminiscences and impressions, inadequate as they are, are likely to throw more light on the workings of the mind and emotions of primitive man than any amount of speculation from a sophisticated ethnologist or ethnological theorist.

Such an autobiography was obtained by the author from a Winnebago Indian and published in volume xxvi of the Journal of American Folk-Lore in 1913. The reception given this first autobiography led to further effort in this direction, the aim being, not to obtain autobiographical details about some definite personage, but to have some representative middle-aged individual of moderate ability describe his life in relation to the social group in which he had grown up. A series of fortunate circumstances enabled the author to secure a rather lengthy autobiography from a member of a very prominent Winnebago family. This is the account here published. The Indian in question was a brother of the Winnebago who had written the earlier autobiography referred to above. The writer is referred to throughout the notes as S. B. No attempt of any kind was made to influence him in the selection of the particular facts of his life which he chose to present. So far as could be ascertained the Indian wrote the autobiography in two consecutive sessions in a syllabary now commonly used among the Winnebago. The translation was made by the author on the basis of a rendition from his interpreter, Mr. Oliver Lamere, of Winnebago, Nebraska.

The autobiography proper closes with Part I. Part II embodies the system of instruction used among the Winnebago and forms a unit by itself. The Indian regarded it as part of his autobiography inasmuch as it represents what he remembered to have heard from his father when he was a young boy.

The various headings have been added by the author. All explanatory matter is included in the notes.

PART I. THE STORY OF MY LIFE

1. EARLY CHILDHOOD

Father and mother had four children and after that I was born, it is said.[1] An uncle of mother's who was named White-Cloud, said to her, ''You are to give birth to a child who will not be an ordinary person.'' Thus he spoke to her. It was then my mother gave birth to me. As soon as I was born and was being washed—as my neck was being washed—I laughed out loudly.

I was a good-tempered boy, it is said. At boyhood my father told me to fast and I obeyed. In the winter every morning I would crush charcoal and blacken my face with it.[2] I would arise very early and do it. As soon as the sun rose I would go outside and sit looking at the sun and I would cry to the spirits.[3]

Thus I acted until I became conscious.[4]

Then there were not as many white people around as there are now. My father always hunted. Our lodge was covered with rush mattings and we had reed mattings spread over the floor. After my father had hunted for a considerable time in one place we would move away. My father, mother, older sisters, and older brothers all carried packs on their backs, in which they carried many things. Thus we would pass the time until the spring of the year, and then in the spring we used to move away to live near some stream where father could hunt muskrats, mink, otter, and beaver.

In the summer we would go back to Black River Falls, Wisconsin. The Indians all returned to that place after they had given their feasts. We then picked berries. When we picked berries my father used to buy me gum, so that I would not eat many berries when I

---

[1] He uses the phrase ''it is said'' for all statements relating to that period of his life of which he has no clear recollection.

[2] i.e., fast.

[3] i.e., make the ceremonial prayer uttered during the puberty fast.

[4] i.e., from that time on he recollects his childhood. However the term *conscious* is not to be taken in any metaphorical sense. To the Winnebago mind anything not remembered is grouped together with non-existent phenomena. An individual is only *conscious* of what manifests its existence to him by means of some inward stirring, be it emotional, intellectual, or physical. For these things that have happened to him in infancy no such manifestation exists and he consequently predicates no consciousness for himself at that period. I do not doubt for a moment that he thinks of these early years of his life as being identical with any unconscious condition occurring in mature life.

was picking.[5] However, I soon managed to eat berries and chew gum at the same time. After a while I learned to chew tobacco and then I did not eat any berries (while picking them). Later on I got to like tobacco very much and I probably used up more value (in tobacco) than I would have done had I eaten the berries.

In the fall of the year we would pick cranberries and after that, when the hunting season was open, I would begin to fast again.

I did this every year for a number of years.

After a while we got a pony on which we used to pack all our belongings when we moved camp. And in addition about three of us would ride on top of the pack. Sometimes my mother rode and father drove the pony when we moved from one place to another.

After I had grown a little older and taller and was about the size of one of my older brothers, all of us would fast together. My father used repeatedly to urge us to fast. "Do not be afraid of the burnt remains of the lodge center-pole,"[6] he would say to us. "Those which are the true possessions of men, the apparel of men,[7] and also the gift of doctoring—these powers that are spread out before you—do try and obtain one of them," he was accustomed to say to us.

I would then take a piece of charcoal, crush it, and blacken my face, and he would express his gratitude to me.

At first I broke my fast at noon and then, after a while, I fasted all night. From the fall of the year until spring I fasted throughout the day until nightfall, when I would eat.[8] After a while I was able to pass the night without eating and after a while I was able to go through two nights (and days) without eating any food. Then my mother went out in the wilderness and built a small lodge. This, she told me, she built for me to fast in, for my elder brother and myself, whenever we had to fast through the night.

There we used to play around. However, before we were able to spend a night at that particular place, we moved away.

---

[5] Cranberry-picking is one of the principal means of support of the Winnebago.

[6] i.e., charcoal with which to blacken one's face while fasting.

[7] i.e., both material and immaterial. He refers mainly to that knowledge which will make a man honored and respected by his fellow men.

"Apparel of men" does not mean clothes, but power and ability; success on the warpath, membership in the Medicine Dance, ability to cure the sick, etc.

"Spread out before you" means "within your power to obtain from the spirits."

[8] No person attempted to fast for twenty-four hours at once without a break.

2. PUBERTY[9]

After a time I passed from this stage of boyhood into another. I began to use a bow and arrow and I spent my time at play, shooting arrows.

Then I found out that my mother had been told, just before I was born, that she would give birth to no ordinary being, and from that time on I felt that I must be an uncommon person.

At about this time my oldest sister married a holy man. My parents gave her in marriage to him. He was a shaman and he thought a great deal of me.

At this stage of life also I secretly got the desire to make myself pleasing to the opposite sex.

Now at that time the Indians all lived in their lodges and the women were always placed in lodges of their own whenever they had their menses. There the young men would court them at night when their parents were asleep. They would then enter these lodges to court them. I used to go along with the men on such occasions for even although I did not enter the lodge but merely accompanied them, I enjoyed it.

At that time my parents greatly feared that I might come in contact with women who were having their menses, so I went out secretly. My parents were even afraid to have me cross the path over which a woman in such a condition had passed.[10] The reason they worried so much about it at that particular time was because I was to fast as soon as autumn came;[11] and it was for that reason they did not wish me to be near menstruating women, for were I to grow up in the midst of such women I would assuredly be weak and of little account. Such was their reason.

After some time I started to fast again throughout the day and night, together with an older brother of mine. It was at the time of the fall moving and there were several lodges of people living with us. There it was that my elder brother and I fasted. Among the people in these lodges there were four girls who always carried the

---

[9] The physiological and other changes at puberty are definitely noted by the Winnebago and a special word is used to cover the years from approximately twelve to twenty.

[10] A very general belief among the Winnebago. Any contact with menstruating women, or even with objects in any way connected with them, will, it is believed, destroy the power of sacred objects or individuals temporarily sacred. Fasting youths were regarded as such.

[11] Fasting always commenced in autumn and never lasted longer than early spring, or until the snakes appeared above ground.

wood. When these girls went out to carry the wood my older brother and I would play around with them a good deal. We did this even although we were fasting at the time. Of course we had to do it in secret. Whenever our parents found out we got a scolding, and the girls likewise got a scolding whenever their parents found out. At home we were carefully kept away from women having their menses, but we ourselves did not keep ourselves away from such. Thus we acted day after day while we were fasting.

After a while some of the lodges moved away and we were left alone. These lodges moved far ahead of us because we ourselves were to move only a short distance at a time. That was the reason the others moved on so far ahead of us. My father and my brother-in-law went out hunting and killed seventy deer between them and in consequence we had plenty of meat.

3. FASTING

When the girls with whom I used to play moved away I became very lonesome. In the evenings I used to cry. I longed for them greatly, and they had moved far away!

After a while we got fairly well started on our way back. I fasted all the time. We moved back to a place where all the leaders used to give their feasts. Near the place where we lived there were three lakes and a black hawk's nest. Right near the tree where the nest was located they built a lodge and the war-bundle that we possessed was placed in the lodge.[12] We were to pass the night there, my older brother and myself. It was said that if anyone fasted at such a place for four nights he would always be blessed with victory and the power to cure the sick. All the spirits would bless him.

"The first night spent there one imagined oneself surrounded by spirits whose whisperings were heard outside of the lodge," they said. The spirits would even whistle. I would be frightened and nervous, and if I remained there I would be molested by large monsters, fearful to look upon. Even (the bravest) might be frightened, I was told. Should I, however, get through that night, I would on the following night be molested by ghosts whom I would hear speak-

---

[12] Every Winnebago clan has at least one war-bundle; most of them have more. The father of S. B. possessed one, and most of the "power" resident in this particular bundle was supposed to have been bestowed by the thunder-birds and night-spirits. Perhaps that is why a black-hawk's nest was selected for the fasting-lodge, the black-hawk being regarded as a thunder-bird, although my interpreter was uncertain about the matter.

ing outside. They would say things that might cause me to run away. Towards morning they would even take my blanket away from me. They would grab hold of me and drive me out of the lodge, and they would not stop until the sun rose. If I was able to endure the third night, on the fourth night I would really be addressed by spirits, it was said, who would bless me, saying, "I bless you. We had turned you over to the (monsters, etc.) and that is why they approached you, but you overcame them and now they will not be able to take you away. Now you may go home, for with victory and long life we bless you and also with the power of healing the sick.[13] Nor shall you lack wealth (literally, 'people's possessions'). So go home and eat, for a large war-party is soon to fall upon you who, as soon as the sun rises in the morning, will give the war whoop and if you do not go home now, they will kill you."[14]

Thus the spirits would speak to me. However if I did not do the bidding of this particular spirit, then another one would address me and say very much the same sort of thing. So they would speak until the break of day, and just before sunrise a man in warrior's regalia would come and peep in. He would be a scout. Then I would surely think a war-party had come upon me, I was told.

Then another spirit would come and say, "Well, grandson, I have taken pity upon you and I bless you with all the good things that the earth holds. Go home now for the war-party is about to rush upon you."[15] And if I then went home, as soon as the sun rose the war whoop would be given. The members of the war party would give the war whoop all at the same time. They would rush upon me and capture me and after the fourth one had counted coup, then they would say, "Now then, grandson, this we did to teach you. Thus you

---

[13] It was customary for parents, generally grandparents, to tell youths who were fasting what kind of an experience they were to expect, and particularly how they were to recognize the true spirit when he should appear and thus guard against being deceived by an evil spirit. Apparently S. B.'s father told the youth in considerable detail what he was to expect on this particular occasion. The supernatural experience given here is peculiar in a number of respects; first, because it contains many elements distinctly intended to frighten the faster, and secondly, because it contains a well-known motif taken from the origin myth of the Four Nights' Wake. In practically all the fasting experiences I collected among the Winnebago the spirits are pictured simply as offering their blessings and having them refused or accepted by the faster. The test theme so prominent here does not occur at all. Apart from these facts, the experience is a good example of the type one would expect to find among the Winnebago, and perhaps the Woodland-Plains tribes in general.

[14] Practically every Winnebago fasting experience contains an attempt of an evil spirit to deceive the faster.

[15] The foregoing gives an excellent idea of how detailed are the instructions given a faster.

shall act. You have completed your fasting.'' Thus they would talk to me, I was told. This war party was composed entirely of spirits, I was told, spirits from the heavens and from the earth; indeed all the spirits that exist would all be there. These would all bless me. They also told me that it would be a very difficult thing to accomplish this particular fasting.[16]

So there I fasted, at the black hawk's nest where a lodge had been built for me. The first night I stayed there I wondered when things would happen; but nothing took place. The second night, rather late in the night, my father came and opened the war-bundle and taking a gourd out began to sing. I stood beside him without any clothing on me except the breech-clout, and holding tobacco in each hand I uttered my cry to the spirits as my father sang. He sang war bundle songs and he wept as he sang. I also wept as I uttered my cry to the spirits. When he was finished he told me some sacred stories, and then went home.

When I found myself alone I began to think that something ought to happen to me soon, yet nothing occurred so I had to pass another day there. On the third night I was still there. My father visited me again and we repeated what we had done the night before. In the morning, just before sunrise, I uttered my cry to the spirits. The fourth night found me still there. Again my father came and we did the same things, but in spite of it all, I experienced nothing unusual.[17] Soon another day dawned upon us. That morning I told my elder brother that I had been blessed by spirits and that I was going home to eat. However I was not telling the truth. I was hungry and I also knew that on the following night we were going to have a feast and that I would have to utter my cry to the spirits again. I dreaded that. So I went home. When I got there I told my people the story I had told my brother; that I had been blessed and that the spirits had told me to eat. I was not speaking the truth, yet they gave me the food that is carefully prepared for those who have been blessed. Just then my older brother came home and they objected to his return for he had not been blessed. However, he took some food and ate it.

---

[16] Some spirits are more difficult to approach than others. The black-hawk, regarded as the chief of the thunder-birds, is one of the most difficult spirits to obtain blessings from. However, blessings from him were quite customary in S. B.'s family.

[17] As we shall see later in connection with S. B.'s conversion to the peyote-religion, he expected some definite inward change. Not receiving it he regarded himself as not having been blessed.

That night we gave our feast. There, however, our pride received a fall,[18] for although it was supposedly given in our honor, we were placed on one side (of the main participants). After the kettles of food had been put on twice, it became daylight.[19]

The following spring we moved to the Mississippi in order to trap. I was still fasting and ate only at night. My brothers used to flatter me, telling me I was the cleverest of them all. In consequence I used to continue to fast although I was often very hungry. However, (in spite of my desire to fast) I could not resist the temptation to be around girls. I wanted always to be near them and was forever looking for them, although I had been strictly forbidden to go near them, for they were generally in their menstrual lodges when I sought them out. My parents most emphatically did not wish me to go near them, but I did nevertheless.

My parents told me that only those boys who had had no connection with women, would be blessed by the spirits. However, all that I desired was to appear great in the sight of the people. To be praised by my fellow-men was all that I desired. And I certainly received all I sought. I stood high in their estimation. That the women might like me was another of the reasons why I wanted to fast. However, as to being blessed, I learned nothing about it, although I went around with the air of one who had received many blessings and talked as such a one would talk.

4. BOYHOOD REMINISCENCES

The following spring I stopped fasting. In those days we used to travel in canoes. My father used to spear fish and would always take me along with him, and I enjoyed it very much. He kept a club in the canoe and after he had speared a fish, I would kill it with the club as it was jumping around in the canoe. Sometimes my mother accompanied us as a third person. She would sit at the rear end and row while father, standing in the prow, speared the fish. I killed all those that were thrown into the canoe with my club.

Sometimes my parents started out without me but I would then cry so bitterly that I always induced them to take me along. Sometimes they would whip me and tell me to go home but I used to follow

---

[18] It was a common practice for the older people to treat the younger men in this way, in order to train them in humility.

[19] There are two meals served during the war-bundle feast, one at about midnight and one about dawn.

them so far that they were afraid to let me go back alone and they would let me ride along with them. Indeed I exerted myself greatly in crying for them, and as I cried and ran after them and followed them very far, I was in the end always taken along.

In those days we always lived in the old-fashioned Indian lodges. In winter our fire was placed in the center of the lodge and my father used to keep it burning all night. When he placed a large log in the fire it would burn a long time. This is what we used to do in the winter.

We were three boys, of whom I was the youngest, and at night we used to sleep together. In cold weather we used to fight as to who was to sleep in the middle for whoever got that place was warm, for while those at either end used to pull the cover from each other, the one in the middle was always covered. Even after I grew up I always took the covering away from whomsover I was sleeping with. I would always fold it under me, for it had become a habit with me to take the cover away from the other person (whenever I slept on the outside).

We always ate out of one dish. Sometimes we did not have enough food on hand and then I would always try to get enough by eating very fast. In this way I always succeeded in depriving the others of their proper portion. Sometimes, on the other hand, I would purposely eat slowly, and then when the others were finished, I would say that I had not been given enough and so I would get some of their food. In this way I developed a habit (that I still have), for I am a fast eater. Even after I grew up, whenever I ate with other people, I always finished sooner than they. (Another habit that I acquired then) was the ability to go without food for a whole day while traveling. I did not mind this in the least for (during my fasting) I had grown accustomed to going without food for long periods of time.

In the summer, at the season when people pick berries, I used to go around visiting, sometimes for a day, sometimes for longer. I would often receive nothing to eat, but I did not mind that. In the summer, when people pick berries, they generally go out in bands and settle here and there. Some were far away from others.

5. COURTING

It was at this time that I desired to court women and I tried it. However, I did not know the proper thing to say. The young men always went around at night courting. I used to mix with the women in the daytime but when I went to them at night I did not know what to say. A brother of mine, the oldest, seemed to know how to do it. He was a handsome man and he offered to show me how. Then I went with him at night. We went to a girl who was having her menses at that time. She was a young girl. When girls get their menses they always have to live apart. It was to such a one that we went. We were very cautious about the matter for the girls were always carefully watched as their relatives knew that it was customary to court them at such a time. (One of the precautions they used) was to pile sticks and branches about the lodge so that it would be difficult to enter. If a person tried to enter he was likely to make a noise moving the branches and this would awaken the people living in the larger lodge nearby and they might run out to see what was the matter.

It was to such a place that we went. After working at the obstacles placed near the entrance for some time, my brother entered the lodge. I went as close as possible and lay down to listen. He spoke in an audible whisper so that I might hear him. Sure enough I heard him. However after lying there for some time I fell asleep. When I snored my brother would wake me up. Afterwards the girl found out and she sent us both away. Thus we acted every now and then.

After a while I entered the lodges myself. We always had blankets wrapped around us and we took care to have our heads well covered (on such occasions).

Sometimes a girl was acquainted with quite a large number of men and then these would gather around her lodge at night and annoy her parents a good deal. We would keep them awake all night. Some of these people owned vicious dogs.

There was one old woman who had a daughter and when this daughter had her menses, she stayed in an oblong lodge with just room enough for two persons. She watched her daughter very carefully. Finally she slept with her. We nevertheless bothered her all the time just out of meanness. One night we went there and kept her awake almost all night. However, just about dawn she fell asleep, so we—there were several of us—pulled up the whole lodge, poles and everything, and threw the poles in the thicket. The next morning the two were found sleeping in the open, it was rumored, and the mother was criticised for being over careful.[20]

The reason why some of the (older) people were so careful at that time was because it had been reported that some young men had forced themselves into lodges where they had not been received willingly.

Once I went to see a young girl and arrived there before the people had retired, so I waited near the lodge until they would go to sleep. As I lay there waiting, listening to them, I fell asleep. When I woke up it was morning and as the people got up they found me sleeping there. I felt very much ashamed of myself and they laughed at me. I was not long in getting away.

We always did these things secretly for it was considered a disgrace to be caught or discovered.

On another occasion, in another place, I was crawling into a lodge when someone woke up as I was about halfway in. I immediately stopped and remained quiet and waited for the people to fall asleep again. However in waiting I, myself, fell asleep. When they woke me up in the morning I was lying halfway inside the lodge, asleep. After waking me up they asked me whether I would not stay for breakfast, but I immediately ran away.

After a while I began going around with some particular girl and I liked it so much that I would never go to sleep at night. My older brothers were very much the same. We used to sleep during the day.

While we were acting in this manner, our parents saw to it that we had food to eat and clothes to wear. We never helped, for we did nothing but court girls. In the fall the Indians used to pick berries after they all came together. We used to help on such occasions. However, we were generally out all night and were not able to do much in the morning. I used to go out courting and be among the lodges all night, and yet, most of the time, I did not succeed in speaking to any of the girls. However, I did not mind that for I was doing it in order to be among the girls and I enjoyed it. I would even go around telling people that I was really keeping company with some of the girls. I used to say this to some of my men associates. In reality, however, I did not get much more than a smile from one or two of the girls, but even that I prized as a great thing.

---

[20] An excellent example of Winnebago viewpoint. To them it appears as reprehensible to be over careful as it would to be over negligent.

6. MY BROTHER–IN–LAW AND HIS FASTING EXPERIENCE[21]

When this was over, we all moved to the hunting grounds and I began to fast (again). I then began to take vapor baths, and also I caused myself to vomit so that I would be purged. My father was a good deer hunter.[22] He was always able to kill many deer and, at times, he also killed some bear.

I had a brother-in-law who thought a good deal of me. He was a holy man and a shaman. One day he said to me, "Brother-in-law, I will bless you. However, you will have to fast for it. I was blessed by four brothers, beings called good giant-cannibals. They said that they had never before blessed any one. They promised me that if I ever came to any difficulty, they would help me. They blessed me with (long) life. Now I will give this blessing to you.[23] If you fast for four nights (without a break), these (giants) will talk to you." Thus he spoke to me. (Then he continued), "There are four brothers and the oldest one is called *Good-giant;* the second one, *Good-heart;* the third one, *Good-as-he-goes-about,* and the fourth one, *Good-where-he-lifts-his-foot-from.* Toward the east, where a promontory is to be found, there they live. Nothing across the large body of water is too difficult for them to accomplish." Thus he spoke.

So when I fasted, I always offered tobacco to them (these spirits) first. Then I would cry to these spirits, but I never fasted over night.

7. A WAR–BUNDLE FEAST[24]

When they were through hunting, my father selected ten deer to give a feast with. The attendants[25] then transferred these deer (to the place) where the people always gave their feasts.

---

[21] This brother-in-law is a very remarkable man. He is one of the few Winnebago living who is supposed to be living his third life on earth. He even claims to be the reincarnated culture hero of the Winnebago, the hare. An account of him is given in "Personal Reminiscences of a Winnebago Indian," Jour. Amer. Folk-Lore, vol. XXVI, 1913. The fasting experience given here is apparently only one of the many he had. He seems to have had a remarkable influence on both S. B. and his brother.

[22] Skill in hunting is one of the traits for which B.'s family was noted among the Winnebago. S. B. in particular inherited this ability.

[23] It was not uncommon for an older man to bestow his blessing upon a younger man. As indicated here, the younger man would in any case have to fast for it. However, it was a foregone conclusion that he would receive it in such a case.

[24] A war-bundle feast consists of two parts, the first part consecrated to the night-spirits (the mythical spirits who are supposed to cause the darkness), and the second part consecrated to the thunder-birds. Both spirits are concerned with the bestowing of war powers. The ceremony consists in the offering of tobacco, buckskins, and eagle-feathers to the various spirits, requesting them to bestow victory in return upon the suppliants.

[25] The attendants are always the male children of the man's sister. Sometimes his brothers help.

I was fasting at that time and ate only in the evenings.[26]   Every evening likewise I would go out and appeal to the spirits before I ate.

Five days before the feast we were to give was ready, I began to fast through the night (as well as the day). The fifth night we went to the feast, together with an older brother of mine. In the daytime I went out into the wilderness and there I appealed (cried) to the spirits. It was not that I was so hungry as that I was very thirsty, for I don't think that either my mouth or my tongue was even moist.

That night we held aloft the deerskins[27] that were to be offered to the spirits, and thus we stood there crying to the spirits. There we wept and those who gave the feast wept with us as they extended their (holy) compassion to us. Then, at midnight, we stood near the war weapons and again raised our cries to the spirits.

Our feast was given in an eight fireplace lodge.[28] The host always sits near the last fireplace, at the east end. That is where we stood crying to the spirits. My older brother fell to the ground.[29] We were stark naked except for our breech-clouts as we did this. After doing this, we put on our moccasins. Then they (sat down) to the feast and the kettles were put on (the fireplace). Then it was daybreak. The feasters sang, singing only dance-songs,[30] however. Then we were to pass the deerskin offerings through the roof of the lodge.[31] My older brother took the lead. I followed and the others came behind me. We all had a deerskin apiece. Only those of us who were giving the feast (had the right to hold) one of the ten deerskins. (A person playing) a flute taken from a war-bundle went ahead of us, and following came the people with (incense) of the burning cedar leaves. We marched around the lodge and my brother and I again made our cry to the spirits. At that time we were naked with the exception of the breech-clouts and the moccasins. Four times we made the circuit of the lodge. Then we passed the deerskins up through the roof of the lodge.

---

[26] i.e., he broke his fast every evening.

[27] Toward the end of the ceremony the deer-skins marked for definite spirits and tied to a stick are held aloft and carried around the lodge in a very dramatic way.

[28] The number of spirits to whom offerings were made varied from feast to feast. An eight-fireplace lodge means that on this particular occasion only eight spirits were propitiated, there always being one fireplace for each spirit.

[29] It was considered a commendable act of piety to fall to the ground exhausted during the performance of a ceremony.

[30] Dance songs were sung at the very end of the ceremony.

[31] This very dramatic rite takes place at the end of the ceremony. The buck-skins are thrown through the roof of the lodge and are supposed to be seized by the spirits to whom they are being offered.

Now the feasters were to eat again. A separate kettle had been put on for us (boys) and we were to eat first. They then called upon a man to eat out of our plate.[32] The name of this man was *Blue-sitter.* He was to eat out of our plate first. He was a holy man, a doctor, and a brave man (one who had obtained war honors). Four deer-ribs were dished out to me[33] in a wooden bowl. Then the one who was to eat out of my plate came and sat down near my dish and began to handle my food. He tore it up in small pieces for me. Then he began to tell me of his blessing.

He told me how all the great spirits had blessed him—the Sun, the Moon, the Thunder-birds, the Earth, the Heaven, the Day, and all the spirits that exist in the heavens. All these blessed him, he said. And the spirits who are on the earth, and those under the waters, all these talked to him, he said. (Thinking) of this power (he possessed) did he partake of my food.[34] I was to go through battle unharmed and I was to obtain some war honor. My children, if I had any, were to enjoy a good and happy life. Thus he spoke.

Then he took a piece of my food in his mouth and placed some in my mouth four times. Then I continued eating and the rest of the feasters began to eat. For quite some time I was not able to eat much. Through it all I was not in the least conscious of any dreams or blessings.[35] (All that I was aware of) was that all the people around were taking pity upon me.

I, on the contrary, had my mind fixed on women all the time. (In doing all these things) I imagined that I had accomplished something great and that I had risen greatly in their (women's) estimation. Even though I tried to render myself pitiable in the sight of the spirits, yet, through it all, my thoughts were centered upon women. I was never lowly at heart and never really desired the blessing of the spirits.[36] All I thought of was that I was a great man and that the women would regard me as a great man.

---

[32] This is regarded as a great honor.

[33] i.e., the poorest meat of the deer. Only the warriors received the choice parts.

[34] i.e., he bestowed some of the power with which he had been blessed upon S. B.

[35] Cf. note 17.

[36] It was absolutely essential, in order to obtain a blessing or derive real advantage from participation in a ceremony to be, as S. B. says, lowly at heart, and also to keep one's attention fixed firmly and exclusively on the fast or the ceremony. Your thoughts are not supposed to wander for a moment. S. B. apparently felt that since his thoughts were so frequently deflected in other directions he could not hope to obtain the desired blessing. He is clearly unfair to himself in claiming that he was only interested in being regarded as a great man. He did not receive any blessing and like a good orthodox Winnebago he explained his lack of success as due to his failure to "concentrate" his attention properly.

8. WANDERING AND HUNTING

After a while I used to get in the habit of going to town. When I got there, I would look into all the barrels to see if there was any food in them, and if there was I would fill my pockets (with whatever I found). My pockets would be full. I used to steal a great deal.

About springtime we always moved away (from town). We would move to whatever place my father intended to trap in, generally to some farming community where there were few Indians. There my mother used to make baskets[37] and sell them to the farmers. We would also circulate a written petition (asking) for any help people cared to give us. Whenever they went on this kind of a (begging) trip, I always went along with them, for sometimes people would take pity on us and at such times they often gave me old clothes. Sometimes we would even get a good meal at some farmer's house. For these reasons, I was always envious of those who went along on such trips.

Occasionally when we got a lot of provisions I had to carry some of them, but I never minded that. In the spring of the year we would begin to shoot with bows and arrows. When the birds returned north, father used to make us bows and arrows and we would shoot birds and sometimes kill many of them. We also used to kill squirrels and my grandmother would roast them for us. My older brother used to be a good shot. I was greatly inferior to him. He often killed pheasants.

Whenever (the older people) went to a large town circulating petitions for help, we youngsters always went along with them. We always took our bows and arrows along with us, for the whites wanted to see how well we could shoot and often placed five-cent pieces on some object at a considerable distance and had us shoot at them. We generally hit a number. I would also let my brother shoot at twenty-five-cent pieces that I would hold between my fingers and he never hit my fingers. We would often make as much as five dollars in this manner and we always gave this money to our parents.

In summer the Indians were accustomed to return from the various places (where they had been camping) to Black River Falls. Therefore we also returned to Black River Falls. In summer we would go out shooting with our bows and arrows and we generally stayed away

---

[37] Basket making, as far as I know, is not a real Winnebago industry. It has probably been recently adopted through the influence of the Ojibwa and Menominee.

all day. At evening when we got home, of course we always expected
to get a scolding so we always had some excuse made up for the
occasion. It really would have been better had we returned earlier
in the day, but we always enjoyed (the hunting) so much that night
would overtake us when we were still a long distance from home.
Often we would not eat anything all day, but we were quite accustomed to that. Sometimes we would go fishing down a stream that
runs nearby and again we would forget (the time) and not return
home until it was very late. We would then get a scolding even if
we gave some sort of an excuse.

9. MY GRANDFATHER ADOPTS ME

My father once gave me away. (On my return one day) I found
my father talking to my grandfather and after a while (I saw) the
old man weep. He had just lost a son, a young man and the last of
his children. They had all died. It was this that they were talking
about. (I heard) my grandfather say finally that he was tired of
living. Then my father, also weeping, called him by his relationship
term[38] and said, "I sympathize with you, for you indeed speak the
truth. Yet, in spite of it all, I want you to live. Here is my son,
my own, and of all my children the one I love best.[39] He is obedient.
He is present here and is listening. He shall be your companion and
as long as you live he will lead you by the hand." Thus he spoke
to him. The old man thanked my father repeatedly.

After that I stayed with him and he thought a great deal of me
and I got along very well in every way. He was a great man, a man
who doctored and had great knowledge of medicine. This he used to
give to the sick. He was also a great medicine man and an old
soldier.[40]

Just about this time a school had been built at Tomah, Wisconsin,
and I wanted very badly to attend it. My grandfather consented and
I went to school there for one winter. In the spring my father came
after me and asked the superintendent whether I could go home for
two weeks and he consented to let me go.

---

[38] i.e., by the term denoting the particular relationship which he bore to the
old man. As a rule, among the Winnebago, a man is called by his cardinal name.

[39] This is not so much conceit upon S. B.'s part as a necessary phrase for his
father to use, in order to show the old man how deeply he sympathized with him
and to what lengths of sacrifice he would go. He would give him the son he
loved best!

[40] By Medicine-man he means here a member of the Medicine Dance. Exactly
what is meant by *soldier* I do not know, but I believe it refers to his having been
in the U. S. army, and not to his being an Indian warrior.

Then father said to me, "My son, your grandfather is dead and they are going to have a memorial ceremony (in his honor) and this is to take place at a performance of the Medicine Dance. Someone, (you know), must take his place (in the ceremony)[41] and they decided that I was to be that one. Now, my son, of all my children I have most control over you. I have never kept anything from you. And you have never willfully disobeyed me. I want you therefore to do me this (favor and take my place). I am getting old and besides I cannot control my desire for drink any longer and under these conditions I would not be able to live up to the teachings of the lodge. I wish therefore to turn my (right) over to you. Do you take your grandfather's place." Thus my father spoke to me.

10. INITIATION INTO THE MEDICINE DANCE[42]

The person who had died and whose place I was to take was an uncle of my father. I was glad of this opportunity for I had always liked the Medicine Dances when I saw them. I had always enjoyed watching from the outside what was going on inside and was always filled with envy. I used to wonder if I would ever be able to be one of them. So, naturally, I was very glad (to join) and anxious as to what (would happen).

We proceeded to the place where the ceremony was to be held, traveling from Tomah to Wittenberg. Sometimes we would have to walk, but I enjoyed it nevertheless. I was very happy.

Finally we arrived at the place and my father explained to the people there that he had turned over his right (to membership) to me and that that was why he had taken me along. They were quite satisfied.

We were to build the lodge immediately, so we went and cut the poles for it, after measuring the length required. Of course we hunted around and got the kind of poles always used for that purpose. Then we made the lodge. We stuck the poles in the earth. We worked together with three old men, brothers of the man who had died. They told me that this ceremony was a holy affair, that it was Earth-maker's play.[43] We always made an offering of tobacco before every-

---

[41] Formerly, practically the only way in which a person could join the Medicine Dance was by replacing some deceased member. On such an occasion the ceremony took on the nature of a memorial performance for the departed and a special place was reserved for the group representing the dead man.

[42] For a description of the Medicine Dance of my paper "The Ritual and Significance of the Winnebago Medicine Dance," Journal of American Folk-Lore, vol. XXIV, no. xcii, 1911.

[43] The Winnebago word means literally "actions, affairs, play," and is the regular ritualistic expression for a ceremony.

thing we did. I, of course, thought that it must indeed be a marvelous thing and I was very happy about it. What I was most eager to see was myself killed and then brought to life again, in the lodge.[44] I also realized that a member of the Medicine Lodge, whether man or woman, was different from a person not belonging to it and I was quite anxious not to be an ordinary person any longer but to be a medicine man.

As soon as we finished building the lodge (the ceremony began) and the first thing the people did was to sing. That first time they kept me up all night and I heard a good deal about sacred affairs. I was not sleepy at any time during the night and I remained this way until morning.[45] I enjoyed it all so much that I did not even go to sleep the next day. The next night they kept me up again, but as before I did not get sleepy. On that night they told me even more things. The third night was the same. Throughout these three nights I did not sleep at all. On the fourth night they sang until morning. On the fifth night they were to have the practice (trial).[46] During the day the people began to come. In the afternoon they went into the sweat lodge. Those (who went in) were all old men. They were the people who had been especially invited with bundles of tobacco. When we came out it was sundown. Then those in the east[47] stopped singing and those especially invited entered.

[44] The shooting ritual is, dramatically, the most important part of the Medicine Dance. It is the Winnebago counterpart to the Central Algonkin *Midewiwin* and is naturally the element that attracts most interest from outsiders and children. There seems to be little doubt that the killing and coming to life again in the shooting ritual was always regarded by the older members of the Medicine Dance as symbolical, and that it was merely a dramatic representation of the belief that all members of the society would receive the gift of reincarnation. Non-members and children, however, always interpreted this shooting ritual literally and the members of the organization, it must be admitted, did everything in their power to create this impression upon the uninitiated.

[45] He is referring here to the so-called "preparatory nights." There are four of them beginning at sunset and generally lasting until midnight or longer. Each one of the four units (called bands) of which the Medicine Dance is composed has its own four "preparatory nights" at which the songs, speeches, etc., to be used at the coming performance are rehearsed. The person to be initiated is, of course, present only at the rehearsals given by the band which he is to join.

S. B.'s insistence that he did not in the least become sleepy is not to be interpreted merely as a sign of marked interest but also as an assurance that he was "concentrating his attention" as was demanded.

[46] The Medicine Dance proper consists of two parts; the first, called "trial," lasting from sunset until sunrise, and the second, the "real" performance, lasting from about seven in the morning until sunset. The main difference between the two divisions is that the speeches are shorter in the former and that the initiation rites take place during the day performance.

[47] The position of honor is given to the band invited first, whose seat is at the eastern end of the lodge. Opposite them, but still regarded as occupying the east, sit the host and his friends. They always enter the lodge first and sing a few songs before the others enter.

Then they took me in charge for the whole night and whenever they talked they would say, "In the morning when he for whom we desire life becomes like us."[48] They meant me and that I would be like them in the morning. So I was indeed extremely anxious for the morning to come. They danced most of the night. They were giving their trial performance.

The next morning just before day, even while the dance was still going on, the one (the leader) in the first and second seat and those at the east end, together with some others, took me out in the wilderness.[49] When we got there, we found a place where the ground had been cleared in the outline of the dance lodge. There they preached to me and they told me that the most fearful things imaginable would happen to me if I made public any of this affair. The world would come to an end, they said. Then again they told me to keep everything secret, and that if I told anyone, I would surely die. After that they showed me how to fall down and lie quivering (on the ground) and how to appear dead.[50] I was very much disappointed for I had had a far more exalted idea of it (the shooting). "Why, it amounts to nothing," I thought. "I have been deceived," I thought. "They only do this to make money," I thought. I also thought then that probably many of the sacred things of which they told me were not true either.[51] However, I kept on and did as I was told to do, for I had been taught to deceive in the ceremony in the wilderness. As soon as I was proficient in the act (of feigning death), we started back.

---

[48] The person to be initiated is known as he-for-whom-we-desire-life. The word for life means literally "light," but in rituals it is always used in this symbolic sense.

"To become like them" means to have been killed and to have come to life again, i.e., to have been reincarnated.

[49] Everything outside of the cleared ground around the village was called wilderness. In this particular case he refers to the cleared ground some distance away from the ceremonial lodge, where the neophyte is to be initiated into the secrets of the shooting ritual.

"Those at the east end" here refers to the members of the host's band.

[50] The person "shot" is supposed to feign death. Those only recently initiated must fall down motionless immediately, but older members have the right to hesitate and to lie on the ground quivering. The right to do this must be bought.

[51] Probably the majority of the people initiated are slightly disappointed but few give expression to it, and I doubt whether S. B.'s disappointment was as intense as he claims here. Certainly his deduction that other ceremonies were as untrue as this one is an afterthought due to the influence of the peyote religion. It is, incidentally, the only case I have found where he was influenced by his later beliefs in interpreting his older life.

They told me that I would become just like them in body, but I did not have the sensation of any change in me.[52] All that I felt was that I had become a (deceiver) in one of Earthmaker's creations.[53]

see p. 67

During the day, at the regular meeting, I did as I had been taught to do. We were simply deceiving the spectators. When we were through, those of my band told me that in two years I would be able to imitate the sounds of animals as much as I wanted to, for I had taken the place of a great medicine man.[54] Those who have the privilege of dancing, obtain it by making gifts to the older members and thus get permission. Those who do not buy or get permission, are not allowed to dance. Similarly in shooting:[55] they are not privileged to extend their arms when they shoot (unless they buy that privilege), but must hold their shooting skins close up to their breasts.[56] The right to drum as well as the right to shake the gourd rattles must be bought before it can be exercised. In fact almost every act is bought before it can be exercised. However I was told that I did not have to do all that, but that I would be a great medicine man immediately.[57] That pleased me. I was given a grey squirrel skin for my medicine bag and they told me that it was alive and that I could make it cry out loud.[58] I had heard them do it and had

---

[52] This is another example of S. B.'s refusal to believe that any change has taken place in him, unless he has some inward sensation of such a change.

[53] The Medicine Dance is, strictly speaking, not the creation of Earthmaker but of the culture hero, Hare. There may be some Christian influence here, for Earthmaker has been generally identified with God. The conservatives have even gone so far at times as to equate Hare with Christ.

[54] By means of whistles, etc., placed inside receptacles made of otter, squirrel, weasel, or other skins, they cause these bags to make noises resembling those made by these animals. It is this spectacular power of the otter-skin bag that greatly impresses the minds of outsiders and children.

S. B. does not mean to imply that he is inheriting any of the powers of the man whose place he is taking, but that he is expected to emulate him.

[55] Not only is an individual ''shot'' when he is initiated, but all initiated members indulge in shooting at each other at certain definite periods during the performance of the ceremony. Only members who have purchased the right to shoot enjoy this privilege. Newly initiated people never have this right, or at least they did not have it in former times.

[56] It is believed that the ability to hold the shooting-bag at arm's length is due to the power ''shot'' into an individual and that therefore a recent member or one recently initiated, who has of course only been ''shot'' a few times, does not possess this power. Consequently all he can do is to keep the shooting-bag pressed closely to his breast.

[57] If he was told this, it can be explained in only two ways: either the ceremony had greatly degenerated, or the relatives of S. B. had made payments sufficient to cover not only the expenses of initiation but also the right to privileges otherwise enjoyed only by members of some standing. I can not help thinking that here S. B. has been led astray by his youthful conceit, and that he is not telling the truth. I know that even eight years ago this would not have been permitted among the Nebraska Winnebago, who are the less conservative of the two groups.

[58] This may be true. It must, however, be taken with caution.

always envied them in this regard. This was another of the things I was anxious to do. Indeed I wondered greatly how this could be done.

The dance was soon over and my father went away and left me there alone; he left me at the home of the deceased man's wife. I did not go back to school but was asked to stay there and do odd jobs for the old woman. So I stayed there all spring.

I had been told that if a person initiated into the Medicine Dance did not regard the affair as sacred, that this was a sign that he was going to die soon. This frightened me a great deal, for I had been thinking of the whole matter in a light manner and I felt that this was an indication that I was really going to die soon. I therefore did my best to consider it a sacred ceremony but, in spite of it all, I did not succeed.

About this time I left for Tomah. It was about the middle of summer (July fourth). I returned and stayed with my grandfather and from that time on was taught by him (details) of the Medicine Dance. (For instance), when I prepared a sweat bath for him, he would teach me some songs. I therefore did this for him frequently. Whenever I prepared such a bath for him, he would be very grateful to me and that is why I did it.[59] Before long I learnt all the songs he knew, so that when I was invited to a medicine dance I would do all the singing and he would only have to do the talking. From that time on I said that it was a sacred affair and I took part in the ceremony for the greatness it possessed.[60] (I boasted of its greatness) in the presence of women in order to make a good impression on them.

About this time I went away with a show to dance. I was fond of dancing and now I had a chance to go around and dance all the time and even get paid for it. I had money all the time. The people with whom I went around never saved anything and were always without funds, for they spent all their money on drink. I never drank. After a while I went with these shows every fall, when the fairs start.

[59] S. B.'s utilitarian interpretation of his actions must not be taken too literally as a rule. However, in this particular case it must be remembered that preparing a bath for an older man was merely one of the accepted ways of informing that you wished to ask him something. Personal regard and affection were shown in other ways. S. B. does not therefore mean, as his words might imply, that he was actuated by purely selfish motives. He was simply doing what custom dictated.

[60] S. B. possessed a very good voice and pronounced musical ability. While the right to sing was considered quite an honor, it often depended largely upon a good voice. S. B. apparently interpreted the privilege as a recognition of his ability and his standing. I doubt whether the others did.

11. MARRIAGE

One fall I did not go and instead I stayed with my grandfather. He told me to get married. I was about twenty-three years old then. I had courted women ever since I was old enough. Every time I did anything I always thought of women in connection with it.[61] I tried to court as many women as I could. I wanted badly to be a beau for I considered it a great thing. I wanted to be a ladies' man.

My grandfather had asked me to marry a certain girl, so I went over to the place where she was staying. When I arrived there I tried to meet the girl secretly, which I succeeded in doing. I told her of my intention and asked her to go home with me. Then she went home for I had met her some distance from her home.

After a while she came back all dressed up and ready. She had on a waist covered with silver buckles and a beautifully colored hair ornament and she wore many strings of beads around her neck, and bracelets around her wrists. Her fingers were covered with rings and she wore a pair of ornamented leggings. She wore a wide-flap ornamented moccasin and in each ear she had about half a dozen ear holes and they were full of small silver pieces made into ear ornaments. She was painted also. She had painted her cheeks red and the parting of her hair red. She was all dressed up.

I went there on horseback. We rode the horse together. We were not going that night to the place from which I had come, because I had previously been asked to sing at a medicine feast by my band (at a place) which was on our way home. I would therefore not go home until the next morning. So on my way there I had the girl hide near the place where we were to have the feast, for we were eloping and that was the custom.[62]

The girl had a red blanket which she was wearing so I had her hide under a small oak bush. It rained all night and the next day. When we were through in the morning, I went to the place (where I had put her) and she was still there, but she was soaked through and through from the rain and her paint was smeared over her face in such a way that one could hardly recognize her. Then we went home. When we arrived home, my grandfather's wife came out to meet us and she helped the girl down from the horse and led her into the lodge. Then we ate. When we were through, the girl took off her clothing

---

[61] i.e., of the impression he would make on women.

[62] Elopement was one of the accepted methods of marriage. It had none of the connotations that the word has among us, for as S. B. indicated the union had been arranged by the old man with whom he was staying.

and gave it to them and they gave her other clothing to wear.[63]   After
the girl had stayed there three nights, she had her menses, so she had
to camp by herself, and there she had to sleep at night.   Then a horse
was given to this girl that I had married.

After a while my grandfather had a private talk with me, and he
said: "Grandson, it is said that this girl you have married is not a
maiden but really a widow, and I am not pleased with it, as this is
your first marriage and you are a young man.   I suppose you know
whether it is true or not, whether she is a maiden or not?"   "Yes,"
I answered.   "You can stop.living with her, if you wish," he said.
So I went away on a visit and from there I went away for good.   After
some time I learned that the woman had gone home.   Then I went
home.   He (my grandfather) was glad that I had not stayed with
her.   "You can marry another and a better one," said he to me, "one
that I shall choose for you, you shall marry."   Thus he spoke to me.
However I said to him, "Grandfather, you have begged women for
me often enough.[64]   Don't ever ask for anyone for me again, as I
do not care to marry a woman that is begged for."   Thus I spoke to
him.   He was not at all pleased at this for he said I was not allowing
him to command me.

12. GOING WITH SHOWS

About this time we went to the Sioux country on a visit.   There
were a number of us.   While there I was given a pony.   I was made
a friend.[65]   When I came home, I used to ride my pony about.   That
same fall a number of people were going out with a show and I went
along with them.   We went to all the large cities in the country.   I
was a good dancer.

There were two women with us; they were grass widows.   After
a while I went with one of them secretly.   She used to drink beer.
After a while I went with the other one also.   They were both accustomed to drink.   They would often ask me to drink but I always
refused.   Finally I married one of the women, but after a while I
also lived with the other one.   I lived with both of them.   We used

---

[63] This bridal costume of the girl was intended as a gift to the husband's
female residents.   As indicated farther on, S. B.'s grandparents reciprocated soon
after by presenting her with a horse.

[64] This rebellion of S. B. would probably not have occurred in former days.   I
never heard the phrase "begging for women" used in this connection before.

[65] This is a real term of relationship, and implies a number of definite mutual
services.

to live in a tipi. They both drank beer and after a while I also drank beer with them. Finally I got to drinking very much and began liking it. However I did it in secret and told them to keep it secret too. Finally, as I used to drink often, a man friend of mine found out about it and then I began to drink with him. Soon the owner of the show discovered that I was drinking. He thought a great deal of me; he thought that my dancing was better than that of the others and when he learned that I was drinking he said he was going to treat me and the two girls to beer some night. I drank a lot of it and I enjoyed it very much. After this I was not able to keep the fact of my drinking secret. I talked very loudly and I was very happy and would sing out every once in a while. Then I drank some whiskey in addition (to the beer) and got drunk. The next morning I said I would never do it again, but afterwards I drank beer in secret.

Finally we stopped and went home. We went across Lake Michigan. It was very stormy and we all got sick. Then my friend said, "Say, let us drink so that we may not get sick," said this man. Then he took out some whiskey. He took out a flask containing two quarts. We drank all night. Very early in the morning we got to Bad Lake (Milwaukee). There we ate our breakfast and again we continued on the train. We were going to Black River Falls and again we drank all day. Then we arrived at Black River Falls. We were still drinking. My relatives saw me and saw that I was drunk. They were very sorry and an older sister of mine wept when she saw me. Then I again made up my mind that I would not do it again. They were paid their annuity money when we got back. After that I did not drink any more (for some time).

After the annuity payment had been (spent), the hunting season was about to open. So I also went to the hunting grounds. I ran away from the women with whom I had been living. I did not continue living with either of them. Then I went to the hunting grounds. There I spent some time hunting. We would start out hunting very early in the morning and would stay out all day and not get home until night. Even if we had run around all day, still we did not take time to have our noon meal. At night, regularly, we would take our sweat baths. We would take them because (they were supposed to act) as charms.[66] I always felt refreshed in the morning after first taking a sweat bath and then bathing in cold water.

---

[66] I think he means "as a means of purification" and to insure success on the hunt.

13. DISSIPATION

Once when I returned (to the camp), I found some other people camping near me. In this camp (I found) my grandfather. He had brought along with him one of the women with whom I had been living. I did not like it. He had indeed brought the older of the two. My grandfather asked me to live with her and I lived with her there at these hunting camps. When the hunting season was over, the woman with whom I was living stayed at my house, but I went home with another woman. This woman (my former wife) remained there for some time afterwards, but finally when she got tired (of waiting for me) she went away.

(About that time) it was reported that she used some medicine on me, this woman that went away. A medicine feast[67] was made and my scalp was operated upon. It was said that she took one of my hairs and put it in a medicine bundle of hers. It was said that she did this in order that I might not leave her, and that if I left her I would get a headache, and perhaps even die. Thus they said. However, this was discovered, and my scalp was operated upon and the hair she had taken was washed with medicine. Consequently nothing happened to me.

After this I began to try and live with as many women as I could, for I had gotten the notion that I was a lady-killer. So I tried to live with as many women as I could.

14. BROTHER'S DEATH

Some time after that my older brother was killed. We had grown up together and were hardly ever separated from each other. I felt heartbroken over the matter. I longed to kill the one who had murdered him. I felt that I would be better off if I were dead myself. That is how I felt. After that I began to drink much more. I wanted to die drinking, that is what I used to say, while I was drinking so heavily. Up to this time I had drunk only secretly, but now I drank heavily and openly. After a while I became a confirmed drunkard. I had by this time quite forgotten that I wanted to die, and really enjoyed the drinking very much.

---

[67] This was a private feast, in no way connected with any important ceremony.

15. DRINKING

About this time I got in the habit of giving women whiskey and getting them drunk, and when I drank and got a woman drunk, then I would steal anything of value she had (on her person). I used to abuse people a great deal. At one time I got to be very handy with boxing gloves. I was never defeated, and that is why I always acted meanly to people. They were always afraid of me for they knew (of my skill). My father was a strong man and had never been defeated at wrestling and my older brothers likewise had never been defeated. For these reasons I was very arrogant. Besides this, I was very big. I am six feet and two inches tall and I weighed two hundred and fifty-five pounds. As a matter of fact I was not strong but merely acted as though I were, for every time I got drunk, I always found myself bound when I got sober. I never stayed with any woman long. All I did was to wander around visiting and doing nothing but drink.

I had four sisters and it was from them and my parents that I received everything I ever possessed, yet I claimed to be a great man.[68] I then had two women staying with me as my wives, and, at one time I had as many as four, two at my parents' house and two staying with other relatives of mine. I wasn't serious with any of them.[69] I lied all the time and I knew how to tell falsehoods. On one occasion four children were born to me and each one had a different mother. Nevertheless even after that I still courted women and kept on drinking.

In the spring there was always work that we could do. We would roll logs down the stream, and drink. I always worked at such occupations, because I could drink a good deal at the same time. Whenever I had any money I would spend it on getting some woman drunk.

16. BOASTING AND BLESSINGS

At the time I began to drink heavily, I began to boast about being a holy man. I claimed that I had been blessed by spirits and I kept on claiming this again and again. I was, of course, not telling the truth, for I had never felt the stirring of anything of that kind within

---

[68] He is not saying this in a sudden burst of remorse, but is simply stating a fact.

[69] i.e., he was not married to any one of them.

me; I claimed it because I had heard others speak of it. Generally when I was just about drunk and on the verge of getting boisterous, yet still conscious of what I am saying, I would make this claim. Then I would say that I was blessed by a Grizzly-Bear spirit, that it had blessed me with the power of being uncontrollable; that I had been taught certain songs and these I would sing at the top of my voice. I used to imitate a grizzly bear and begin to exert my power. Then the people (around) would (try to) hold me. It generally required a large number of people to control me.[70]   Now I thought this (exhibition of mine) an act worthy of praise.

After a while I began to claim that I was blessed by many spiritual beings. Some time after I said that I was one of the giant beings called *Good-Giants*,[71] that I was the second-born one of these and that my name was *Good-Heart;* that I had become reincarnate among human beings, dwelling with them.[72]   All this I would claim and they would believe me.

17. THE EFFECT OF A PRETENDED BLESSING

Once when I was on a drinking spree, I visited a certain lodge. There I found a girl whom I was accustomed to call ''niece'' and whom I always used to tease.[73]   I used to call her, in jest, ''mother,'' ''sister.'' This particular time, (when I came), after I had been offered food and eaten it, I also began to tease the girl sitting there. Then the other women (present) said to me, ''My younger brother, your niece is really in a condition to excite your compassion; she is, indeed, practically about to face death, for she is going to be confined, and, on such occasions, she barely manages to escape death.''

---

[70] All the details of this blessing are quite correct. He may be lying, as he claims, but I suspect that there was more in it than that. The power of being uncontrollable was the characteristic gift of the grizzly-bear.

[71] In the light of this statement, remembering that his brother-in-law had actually turned over to him the blessings he had obtained from these cannibal spirits, it seems reasonable to believe that S. B. is unjust to himself in insisting that he lied about these blessings. It is clear that he did not obtain what he considered the only warrant for their truth, the stirring of something within him, but he doubtless did all that was technically required of him, and therefore his fellow Indians believed him. Theoretically, S. B. was quite right in insisting upon this ''thrill,'' because so the old people taught, but the more practical-minded Winnebago never waited for it. This the older people realized, for in the ''teachings'' given the children, as S. B.'s father clearly says in Part II of this memoir, provision is made for those who are not able to receive blessings.

[72] I believe that in making this claim, a rather unusual one, he was probably influenced by his brother-in-law (cf. 21) Who claimed to be the reincarnated Hare. Although S. B.'s brother-in-law was a well known man, his claim was not accepted by most people, and, of course, in the case of S. B. such a claim probably met with no acceptance at all.

[73] i.e., with whom he was on terms of *joking relationship*. This relationship existed between a man and his *maternal* uncle, his daughters and his daughters' daughters ad infinitum.

"Ho, very well," said I, "my elder sister, (this time) my niece is not going to suffer. Up above in the heaven there exist four women, sisters, and these blessed me, telling me that if ever I called upon them for help, they would help me. Now to these I will offer tobacco and when she (my niece) is ready (about to be delivered), she must ask them for help." Thus I spoke to her. The woman thanked me then. However I told a tremendous falsehood. I said all this because I was hungry. Then they gave me enough to appease my hunger. I had nothing else to say.

Some time after this I saw them in town. The woman came over to me (and said), "My younger brother, it is good. Your niece is in the (excellent) condition you claimed she would be; she is very well indeed. She has just given birth to a child. Within three days of her delivery she was able to chop wood. Never before had that happened to her. It is good. As soon as the annuity payment is made you may have the child's share for drink." Thus she spoke.

I was surprised. Perhaps I am really a holy man, I thought.[74]

After (this incident) I boasted even more (of my powers), for now I really thought I possessed sacred power. I therefore talked as those do who have knowledge of all the spiritual beings that exist. I also spoke with the authority of a great medicine man.[75] I used to do the singing for my band, for I had a deep bass voice, and they therefore (liked to have me) do their singing. Sometimes I would be given offerings in kind to make a kettle of food.[76]

I always drank a good deal whenever a Medicine Dance was given and (frequently) I would knock people unconscious, even those in the vicinity of the camp.

---

[74] This interesting experience, to my mind, sheds great light upon the whole question of the relationship of the individual to the spirits and the nature of the efficacy of their power. It seems clear that S. B. had not obtained this particular power either by fasting, or through purchase, or as a gift. Apparently he had heard about these particular spirits and their functions. That, in part, his desire to appear important and powerful played a role here, there is little question, but that seems to me of minor importance. He wanted to help, and, while strictly speaking he had no right to call upon spirits who had not blessed him, yet every Winnebago had more or less the right to offer tobacco to any spirits he wished. Whether it would be of any avail was I believe a moot question. To the practical minded among them there seems to have been the feeling that if you were to offer tobacco and murmur the proper prayers and be sincere in your desire for help, although even the latter was not absolutely necessary, the spirits would be likely to help you; that, as a matter of fact, they are constrained to help you. All this S. B. did. His success would have been accepted by any Winnebago as a proof that the spirits had hearkened; for some it would have been regarded as a proof that he had been blessed. S. B. with his insistence upon an "inward thrill" was genuinely surprised, and was apparently beginning to realize that power from the spirits could be obtained in another way.

[75] i.e., with the authority of a member of the Medicine Dance.

[76] i.e., to make a feast and offer tobacco to the spirits.

18. WITH A CIRCUS

Once we went out hunting in the fall of the year. We killed some game. We used to sell the hind quarters of the deer we killed. Sometimes we would ship them away to Chicago. We were, of course, only permitted to hunt for thirty days. If anyone hunted longer than that, he would (of course) be arrested (if caught). Such was the law. But in spite of the law we hunted beyond the prescribed time on the theory that the law was only meant for the whites. We shipped some more (deer) away and were detected. We had shipped deer and as a result my elder brother and myself were arrested and taken to court, where we were told that we would have to spend sixty days in jail. We were then put in jail. There we stayed. During our imprisonment I never had my hair cut and from that time on I wore my hair long. I told people that he whom we call Trickster[77] had instructed me to do this and that he had blessed me, and I told my elder brother to do the same thing (i.e., to let his hair grow) and (Trickster) would bless him with (long) life. From that time on I wore long hair.

After a while my hair grew very long. Then I went out among the whites with a show. They (the people) liked me very much because I had long hair and I was well paid. During all that time I drank. After a while I learned to ride a bicycle and I also learned to ride wild horses. I always used to say that I was a cowboy, because I wore my hair long. I used to ride many vicious horses and many times I was thrown off. I did all this because I was wild, not because I (really) was an expert. (At one time) I took part in a bicycle race on a race track. I was in full Indian costume and wore long hair.

This (show) played at St. Paul, Minn. I took part in it every summer. Soon I became acquainted with many people and they always asked me to come again. Finally I would not even return to the Indians in winter.

One season someone asked me to get together a number of Indians of whom I was to be in charge. I was told that I would be allowed ten dollars a week for each Indian and that I could pay them whatever I liked. I was quite satisfied, for I could pay them about five dollars

---

[77] In former times the Indians always wore their hair long and the older conservative Winnebago still do.

The Trickster was not one of the bona fide spirits of the priests' ''pantheon,'' but he was popular with the people, although blessings from him are not common. Offerings were, at times, made to him at the war-bundle feast.

a week and thus make some money, I thought. So I persuaded a number of people to go along with me and we all started. We rode to the place from which (this man) had written. From there we started out and went to the fairs. We never made any money and finally we went bankrupt. The man could not even pay me. We felt angry and went to another show with whose manager I was acquainted. We were to divide the receipts.

We were now about to give our show at a certain place for the last time, for the cold weather was setting in. So it was our last day. (On that day) one of the boys with me told me that someone had struck him. I got angry. I told him to point out to me the offender if he could remember him. Just then the person appeared and I tried to strike him but he ran away so I did not succeed in knocking him down. However I struck him in the face with a drumstick. In the evening it was said that, "the man whom one of you struck says that after the show is over this evening, he will kill a certain Indian." "Let him know that perhaps he also is subject to death," I said. "I, also, am anxious to get hold of him." After the show was over, we put on our citizen's clothes and took our handbags. "None of you must go out alone," I said, "for you might get hurt." One of the boys was on horseback, for he wanted to water his horse and was taking it to a trough. But there his pony was taken away from him and he had to return without it. His hat was taken away from him so he returned bareheaded. (As a matter of fact), he barely escaped with his life. "Let us go back," said I. I told the other boys to go on and not to worry about us. I gave them my valise to take along. Then we returned to the place where the boy had been attacked. Before we got there, this same boy was set upon with clubs. We were right in a big crowd of white people. On they went shouting and chasing him. Then they saw me and went at me. I fought them with my bare fists. I just whirled from one side to the other. I was surrounded by them. Whenever anyone got near enough to me, I struck him. They would stand off and strike me with their clubs. Then I started to run and I was hit on the head but not knocked unconscious. Now I was angry and I struck out at all those within my reach. Had I had a weapon I would have killed some of them. Finally several fell upon me. Again I was struck on the head with a club and my head was entirely covered with blood. Then I started for our show tents for they had not been moved yet. Just then the man who had started all the trouble came toward me with a hatchet. I started

for him and when I met him and he raised his hatchet, I struck him
and knocked him down, for I hit him straight in the mouth.

Just then a policeman came toward us and took me and led me
to our show tent. I was covered with blood. The women all wept
and told the policeman who I was, that it was not my fault for I had
not been drinking. They took me to the jail. Then I told the policeman that we ought not to be locked up, for we had not been the ones
who had started all the trouble. Not we but the others should be
locked up. It was this other one who had been drinking. Thus I
spoke to him. "You are right, I will go and look for your things.
But you ought not to be on the street for you have injured many
people.[78] You had better stay in jail for a few hours, for they are
watching me. Now I'll go for your pony and then you can do whatever you like," he said. Then they put me in jail and there I found
the other Indian with whom I had started out. "Well, it is good.
I thought they had killed you," he said. "Well, how many did you
kill?" he asked me. "I didn't kill anyone," I answered. "It is good,
for I thought that they had either killed you or you had killed them,"
he said.

Then I washed the blood from my head. The policemen returned
and brought my pony with them, and also my hat. Then they said,
"You are to go right home. It is true that you have been unfairly
dealt with, but this is a regular fair town and if any trouble starts in
the courts from this affair, it will hurt our fairs in the future. We
shall therefore not go to law about it. The man who started this
trouble is the owner of a large hotel and one of his men owns a trot-
ting horse. These are the men who started the trouble. Now you
have knocked out all the teeth of the hotel-keeper and we do not
know whether he will live or not; and you have bruised the other
person's head badly. So you had better go home," he said.[79]

From there we started for our home. My partner rode a pony
and rode through the middle of the town. I went in the same direction. He was afraid to go through the crowd of white people. A
policeman took us out to the edge of the town. There we told him
that we wanted some whiskey. So he went into a saloon and brought
us two quarts of whiskey. From there we went home. My partner
was riding a two-year-old pony and a small one, but nevertheless we

---

[78] Whether true or not he naturally would insist that he had hurt a number
of people.

[79] In all likelihood this speech is slightly colored in order to motivate S. B.'s
willingness to depart and not continue the fight.

both rode on it. Every time a team came up behind us, we were afraid. After we had been drinking, however, then we said that if (the fight) were to occur again, we would (surely) kill someone, for we felt sorry (at its termination). However no one pursued us.

In the neighborhood some Indians lived and we went to them that very night. When I told them about it, they were frightened, for they thought that (these people) might come out there to fight. These people therefore moved away the next morning. The other man and I took up their trail and followed them. We still rode the little pony together. We had plenty of whiskey along with us. At night we came upon their camps again. They were really trying to get away from us for they were afraid that someone might still come out and fight with us.

There I found out that my relatives were camping nearby so I went over to them. They felt very sorry for us. They were working there, digging potatoes. There were many Indians working there. I stayed at that place, at a woman's house.

19. CONTINUED DISSIPATION

As I stayed there, I was one day handed a paper by a woman. She told me she was married at the place where she was staying, but if I came over, she would do whatever I said. I told the woman with whom I was living about it and she said, "Go after her that I may have her as a companion." Her father had a horse and on it I rode over to the woman's house. I went and secretly watched the people digging potatoes, for their camp was nearby. The man who was living with this woman was also living with another woman.[80] The woman I came for was in the camp. I went over to her secretly. When I got there she began to get ready. Then we rode on the pony and we (happened) to run past the place where the man was working. He chased us, but we got away from him. I (soon) arrived home and the other woman, indeed, received her willingly. They would sleep with me alternately.

When our work was finished there we went to the place from which we had originally come, and just as we reached home, our annuity payment was made. The superintendent of the Wittenberg school made the payment. As soon as we got home, one of the women with whom I was living was taken away from me. She went and lived with

---

[80] Wife stealing is quite common now. It was rare in former times.

another man. When the payment was over, the superintendent went to a place called Yellow-water (Necedah) to pay these people, and then he was to go to Red-Hill. I went along, for I was "chasing up the payment."[81] There I deceived many women and thus I obtained quite a sum of money. Then I started off with a number of other young men. By this time I was spending all my time drinking.

I got on the train at night. At a place called Honsa, we had to change cars. From there we rode on a freight car. When we had gone only a short distance the conductor saw us and put us off. We were all drinking. One of us had lost his hat and was going along bareheaded. We walked into some pasture and there found some dry wood, with which we built a fire. We were going to sleep there. We had all had plenty of whiskey. Late at night we became thirsty so we looked around for water. We found pools of water here and there and out of these we drank. Then we went to sleep. The next morning when we woke up we saw a good well near us, but we had drunk out of the water and mud in which the pigs had wallowed.[82]

In the morning when the train arrived, we all boarded it. We got to our destination. There we found many people drinking and a lot of noise. That was what I was looking for. Whenever I saw a person drunk I would steal whatever he had, for that was what I was (a thief). If I saw a woman drunk, I would steal her, for that was what I was (an adulterer).[83] What I was looking around for mainly was to induce a woman to live with me, for in this way I was able to get money from her. If any woman wanted to marry me while staying with me, she would give me all the money she had. This is the kind of work I was doing. I would often, in this way, induce two or three (women) to live with me.

After finishing at Necedah, the superintendent always went to Tomah to make the payment, and when finished there he would proceed to Black River Falls. At Black River Falls the last payment was made, and for that reason, that was always an extremely noisy place. All who liked this kind of life, all who used to chase around for the fun of it, (would be there). There marriages would get badly

---

[81] This disreputable custom is still in full swing.

[82] He does not relate this incident to point a moral but simply as a fact, and possibly as a humorous occurrence.

[83] Here his present religious affiliations have prompted him to call attention to this particular sin, for it is one of the sins the peyote religion specifically condemns.

mixed up, the stealing of one another's wives, fighting, robbery of one another's money. Even those married people who had been faithful to each other until then, would become unfaithful on this occasion. Many would be hurt here. And when the last payment was over, all those who had not spent their last cent on drink would begin gambling and the men and women would play poker. Only when our last cent was gone, would we stop and settle down. Many of us were generally left without enough money to go home.[84]

20. I COUNT COUP ON A POTTAWATTOMIE

I never married any woman permanently. I would live with one woman for a while and then with another. Sometimes while I was living with a woman, I would return after a short absence to find her living with another man. Thus I acted.

My father brought me up and encouraged me to fast that I might be blessed by the various spirits and (thus) live in comfort. So he said. That I might obtain war honors, that I might not be like one who wears skirts (effeminate), thus my father raised me. For that reason he had me join the Medicine Dance, lest in life I be ridiculed by people. To lead a sober and sane life (my father taught me), and when I lived with my grandfather, he said the same. They encouraged me to give feasts and ask the (spirits) for war honors.[85]

At that time I had a comrade[86] and one day he said to me, "We have been thinking of something (of late, haven't we?) We ought to try and obtain some external emblem of our bravery. Do we not always try to wear feathers at a warrior dance?[87] Well, let us then try to obtain war honors, so that we can wear head ornaments." Thus both of us said. We both liked the idea. We decided to go (in search of war honors). We meant to kill an individual of another tribe, we meant to perform an act of bravery. Finally we started out. There were four of us and we went to a place frequented by

---

[84] This saturnalia has developed only in recent times. I know of nothing to suggest that we are here dealing with an old survival.

[85] Here all the Winnebago ideals are mentioned and the cardinal point of their exhortations to the younger people brought out—"do all that I tell you lest people ridicule you."

[86] i.e., friend. Cf. note 65. A man had to share every danger with his friend and was not supposed to return from any enterprise on which his friend had been killed. A very similar relationship existed between a man and his maternal uncle.

[87] Indicating that they had been on the war-path and killed an enemy or counted coup.

other tribes. We took the train, carrying some baggage. We had ropes along, too, for we intended to steal some horses as well as kill a man, if we met one. Horse stealing was regarded as a praiseworthy feat and I had always admired the people who recounted the number of times they had stolen horses, at one of the Brave dances. That was why I did these things.

We proceeded to a place where horses belonging to men of other tribes used to abound. Just as we got there we saw the owner of these horses and we killed him. My friend killed him. Then we went home and when we got there I told my father about it secretly. I said to him, "Father, you said it was good to be a warrior and you encouraged me to fast, and I did. You encouraged me to give feasts, and I did. Now we have just returned from a trip. We were looking for war honors and the young people (who accompanied me) decided that I should lead them. I told them that it was a difficult thing to lead warriors, my father had always told me; that I had always understood that one led a band of warriors only in consequence of a specific blessing; that I was not conscious of having received such authority." Thus I spoke. "However, they made me an offering of tobacco as they asked me, and I accepted the tobacco saying that I would at least make an offering of tobacco (for them). Then I offered tobacco to the Thunder-birds and asked them for rain, that we might walk in the power (protection) of rain. This offering we made in the morning and it rained all that day. Then we went to the place where we knew we could find horses. When we got there, we met the owner of the horses and spoke to him. We went with him to a carpenter shop nearby and there we killed him. I counted coup first and I announced my name as I gave a war whoop. I shouted '*Big-Winnebago* has counted coup upon his man.'[88] Then the others counted coup. Then we searched his pockets and found some medicine and money in them. The money we divided among ourselves. After that we cut out his heart, for we had heard that hearts were used for medicine. For that reason we cut out his heart. He had a gun too, and this is it, one of them said. Hide it away, said I to him."

Then my father said to me, "My son, it is good. Your life is no longer an effeminate one. It is this way that our ancestors encouraged us to live. It is the will of those (spirits) in control of war that has led you to do this. On your own initiative you could not possibly

---

[88] A person always received a new name, which he gave himself, on counting coup for the first time.

have done it.''[89] Thus he spoke. "However we had better not have a victory dance. We have the honor nevertheless. We have to be careful about the whites," he said. "In the old time we were at liberty to live in our own way, and when such a deed as yours became known, your sisters would rejoice and dance, it has been said.[90] However now the law (of the whites) is to be feared. In due time you will get a chance to announce your feat, and then you may wear a head ornament,[91] for you have earned one for yourself," he said.

21. TRIP TO NEBRASKA

Soon after this I was to go to Nebraska. I once had a child, a boy, who had died when he was two years old. His mother's father then adopted one in his place. The child was a Menominee. So I went there for I was the (adopted) father of the boy and he was (regarded as) my son, for he had been adopted to fill my dead son's place. At the dance given when a person is adopted to fill a dead person's place, I gave him a horse. The dance was a Sore-eye Dance.[92] These (people) gave me some beaded bags, two boxes of maple sugar,

---

[89] i.e., some spirit must have directed you. This would be the religious Winnebago's interpretation of most acts. In this particular case the old man is trying to reassure S. B., who insisted, as we saw a few lines above, that he had received no blessing and was conscious of no authority to lead a war-party. To the old man, and he typifies the average Winnebago, two things were of paramount importance: first, that S. B. had succeeded, and secondly, that S. B. had made an offering of tobacco to the thunder-birds and uttered a prayer asking them for protection. To an old pious Winnebago such as S. B.'s father at this time was, it was clear that the thunder-birds would listen to his son's prayer for, first, the family belonged to the thunder-bird clan, secondly, various members had received blessings from them and, thirdly, the clan war-bundle which they possessed had been bestowed upon an ancestor, not so many generations back, by the thunder-birds. There was, as a matter of fact, a legend current in the family to the effect that this ancestor was the son of a human being and either a thunder-bird or a night-spirit, both of them spirits presiding over the destinies of war. In addition to having his son succeed the thunder-birds had answered by sending rain in response to S. B.'s prayer. S. B. himself probably accepted this as "authority" to proceed.

[90] On the return from a successful war party those who had counted coup were given presents of strings of wampum, and it was customary to give these to one's sisters who hung them around their necks. The women, especially the sisters wearing their war trophies, also danced around the post where the victory dance was held.

[91] i.e., a feather in your hair. Cf. note 87. These war exploits were always announced at certain dances or at the Four Nights' Wake, but never at the Medicine Dance.

[92] As a rule a special adoption feast was given on such an occasion. Apparently, however, other dances could be substituted.
The Sore-Eye dance is regarded as one of the oldest of their ceremonies as well as one of the most sacred. Its real name is "the dance of those who have been blessed by the night-spirits," and it is a secret organization. S. B.'s father and brother belonged to it. S. B. does not mention his having joined it and I do not believe he was a member.

etc. Just when I was about to start out for Nebraska he came and brought me some things. I was at Wittenberg then. I was living there with a woman. Then I went to Nebraska. The woman let me take many things along with me, so that I might give them to my relatives when I got to Nebraska and get horses in return for them.

When I started I stopped off at Black River Falls. I went to a woman with whom I used to live in order to take her along with me, but she refused. I had gone to her while I was drinking. So I had to go on alone. I had my gun along with me. I arrived in Nebraska in midsummer (celebration time).[93] I arrived very early in the morning and there I met a man whom I had once known. He used to go about with me. There were many people. We sat somewhat away from them and the man and his wife drank with me. Then I told them what I had done and he shook hands with me[94] and said that he (too) had counted coup and that he would wear a head ornament. Then they took me to the place where they lived. They hauled my things for me.

The next morning the Nebraska Winnebago were going to celebrate. They were to come together for a week. They had a large gathering. The people with whom I was staying went out and camped with those at the gathering. Two men arrived there. They recognized me and shook hands with me. They were riding in a buggy and I got in with them. They took me far away. On the road they stopped. We got out of the buggy and took out a jug containing four quarts of (whiskey). Then they had me drink with them. After that they brought me back to the gathering and there I met an uncle of mine to whom I presented the gun. He was quite delighted.

It was a large gathering and we danced every day. I got ready also and danced, and there I gave away my things.[95] I received two ponies and a harness and a top buggy. That much I was given. After (the celebration) I remained there for a long time. I even got married there. I kept on drinking all the time. It was then that a nephew of mine begged me to give him my buggy.[96] [A nephew has

[93] While this celebration has now been merged generally with the fourth of July festivities, it is really old and was part of a number of festivities that took place at this time, the principal one of which was the feast given by the chief of the tribe to his fellow men. Comparatively little is known of this feast today.

[94] Shaking hands is a custom recently adopted.

[95] I presume he is referring to the Herucka dance (the Omaha Grass dance) where it was customary to give things away. These dances were always attended by visitors from other tribes.

[96] Not a nephew in our sense, but one who called S. B. *hide′k‘*, and since this relationship is hereditary there were doubtless quite a number of people to whom he bore this relation.

the privilege of asking his uncle for anything and (the uncle) must give it.[97] In return, the uncle can compel his nephew to work for him at any time.][98]

Some time after that I went to visit an uncle of mine.[99] He said, "Nephew, tomorrow they are going to have a Medicine Dance. To-night they are going to have the trial dance. Your aunt is going to buy provisions for the meal and you may go along with her." So I went with her. When we got to town we drank. On the following day it was rumored that the woman and myself were missing.[100] The buggy we were riding in was broken up; my hat was gone and my trousers were torn open. I immediately went back to the place where I had come from, although the Medicine Dance was taking place. The woman, it was said, was still missing. Then I returned to the place where I had been staying and remained there all day. I got very tired. In the morning I mounted a horse and went to the store. When I got there I was arrested. They asked me what I was doing there. "I am not doing anything; I'm merely visiting," I said. Then the one in charge of the law said, that I was to pay ten dollars and that if I did not do so he would send me away. So there I sold the horse I had ridden on. It was a good horse and I got twenty-five dollars for it, out of which I paid the ten dollars. Then the lawyer said, "You have committed many crimes and you had better go to the place from which you came. If you stay here any longer we will have to lock you up."

I left that same day. Two old men were going to Wisconsin and I went with them. They did not know how to speak English, so they took me as an interpreter. I left one of my horses there in pasture. These men were very fond of whiskey and I bought whiskey for them all along our route. After some time we arrived in Wisconsin at the season of cranberry-picking. I was just about drunk when we got there. When we got near our home I said to the men that they should come and visit. This I said and then gave a whoop.

---

[97] It might be added that while this right existed theoretically, no properly brought up nephew would make any impudent demand of his uncle or vice versa.

[98] This was apparently added for my benefit. As a rule S. B. explained nothing of his own accord.

[99] Cf. note 96.

[100] The woman was the wife of his uncle *hide'k'* (his mother's brother) and may very well have been a young woman. As his *hide'k'* 's wife, any transgression of this kind would be regarded even now with marked disfavor, and was probably unthinkable in former times. Any transgression with his real aunt (from our viewpoint) would be unthinkable even now, in spite of the complete breakdown of all their moral standards.

22. I HAVE A QUARREL WITH A WOMAN

My father and mother and a woman with whom I was living when I left, met me. They were very glad (to see me). There were many people camping when I got home. The woman fixed a bed for me, gave me some food to eat and told me to lie down. But I, instead, went out and made inquiries about a woman with whom I used to live, (and found out that) she was still there. To her (lodge) I went and slept. In the morning the other woman was angry; nevertheless the next night I slept there again. Late that night someone woke me up. "Come out," the voice said. I went out with a blanket around me and there was the other woman (my wife). She it was who had called me. She said, "In the morning the annuity payment is to be made at Necedah. I am going there tonight. I want you to go with me." "I haven't any money," I said to her. "As though you ever had any money of your own, when you did anything!" But I refused to go. She persisted and finally I went back and lay down. After a while she came there and she hit me very hard and she called me names. She kicked me and she pulled my hair. Indeed she did all sorts of things to me. "If I had something with which to kill you, I would kill you," she said. Then I got angry and she stopped bothering me and went away.[101]

23. I GET DELIRIUM TREMENS AND SEE STRANGE THINGS

During the cranberry-picking season I drank all the time and after that again "chased payments." I continued drinking. Finally all the payments had been made and I went to Black River Falls. I was entirely without money. I was supposed to go back to Wittenberg but I did not have the fare. I went back to the Indians and stayed all night. In the morning I was sick. I was shaking (from head to foot). When I tried to drink coffee, I would spill it. When I lay down I would see big snakes. I would cry out and get up and then when I was about to go to sleep again, I would think that someone had called me. Then I would raise my cover and look around, but there would be nothing. When the wind blew hard (I seemed) to hear singing. These (imaginary people) would spit very loudly. I heard them and I could not sleep. Just as soon as I closed my eyes, I would begin to see things. I saw things that were happening in a distant country.[102]

---

[101] A man can not of course strike a woman.
[102] This was usually regarded as a gift greatly to be prized.

I saw ghosts on horseback drunk. Five or six of them were on one horse and they were singing. I recognized them, for they were people who had died long ago. I heard the words of their song, as they sang:

"I, even I, must die sometime, so of what value is anything, I think."[103]

Thus they would sing and it made a good song. I myself learned it and later on it became a drinking song and many people learned it. I liked it very much.

The next morning I rode on a train and (after a while) we came to a town. Two days after this I stopped drinking and kept it up through the whole winter, for I was unable to drink. I would vomit every time I drank beer. So all winter I did not drink, and it was not until the following summer that I began again.

24. I AM ARRESTED AND I CONFESS

Two years elapsed. Then, after some time, it was reported that the men who were responsible for the disappearance of the man of another tribe (the Pottawattomie) had been discovered. So I learned, it was said. One of those involved had been to Nebraska and had announced it in recounting acts of bravery at a Brave Dance. So it was rumored. He had also announced it at a death wake.[104] It was thus that the facts had been learned.

Then after a while, in winter, while I was living in the forest chopping wood, two men came there one night. They were officers. They mentioned a man's name to me and asked me if I knew him. "Yes," I said. "Well, let us go to town and there we want to ask you something," they said. Then they told me to get ready. I got ready and then they had me ride in a wagon they had. Then the men asked, "Did Peter kill this man? Do you know?" "I do not know,"

---

103 Songs are frequently composed in this way. Occasionally a man composes a song quite unconsciously. My interpreter related to me that once while riding from Laredo, Texas, to Kansas City he got drowsy and kept time to the noise of the wheels by humming what he thought was a well-known Winnebago peyote song. On his return to Winnebago he kept on humming and singing it and was asked by his friends where he had picked up that new song. Only then did he realize that he had unconsciously composed a new song. Of course these songs all conform to a certain type; S. B.'s doubtless conforming to the accepted drinking song and my interpreter's to the peyote song.

104 Well-known warriors were always invited to a death-wake so that they might recount their war exploits and place at the disposal of the soul whose death is being commemorated, the souls of the people he has killed, in order that they may take care of him and help him safely to his journey's end in spirit-land.

I said to them. Then he told me from what source he had learned it, and asked me, "Did you ever hear anything about it?" "No," I answered. "Did you know that this man was missing?" he asked. "I did hear that a man had been missing but as I did not know him, I did not give the matter much thought," I said to him. Then he said, "It has been discovered that Peter did it. Do you think they are right about it?" "I don't believe a word of it," I said. Then he said, "If you continue to say that you do not know anything about this case, I will not let you go home. You shall go wherever Peter goes. We have found out that you were with him and that is why we are doing this. If you do not tell us you will never get out of prison. That is the penalty (for what you have done). If you tell us, you can get away and you will be a witness and can then go home." "I want to get home, and whatever I can do to get home, I will do. But I don't know anything about this matter. You can speak about what you know. (That) I also can do. I do not want to be locked up," I said.

Then we arrived in town. Then he took me into a hotel, and asked me if I knew the murdered man's brother. "Yes," I said to him. Then we went inside and there we found him. The man greeted me and said, "If you know about this affair and confess, we will not lock you up. You will be one of the witnesses. Even if it turns out that you were with him, we will not lock you up (under those conditions). I am not deceiving you. This one here listening to us, is of the same opinion as myself." Then he said, "Sam, I am acquainted with your father. He is a fine old man. Even if you were along with this man (Peter) I will not have you locked up, if you confess. It is merely because Peter is a bad man that I want to know of it." "He must be telling the truth," said I to myself. "I'm going to tell." I thought that they might not take me back with them, in that case. Then I said, "I know of it. I saw him when he killed him." "Good," said they. "How did he do it?" I told it in detail. "Good!" they said. They thanked me. Then the officer took me outside; he took me to jail and he put me in, and saying, "The train will soon be ready," he went out.

(In the jail) I found the man (Peter). "What did they say to you?" he asked. "They did not say anything to me," I said. "They asked me very many questions," (Peter said). They asked me if you had done it and they said that if I told them, they would let me go home. I told them however that I did not know anything." Thus

I spoke. "They asked me the same things, and I also told them that I did not know anything," I said. "That is good, for without witnesses, they have only hearsay evidence, and they can not hold us," said he. "Anyhow, the man we killed was crazy and his brothers hated him. They used to ask me to kill him. That's what they once asked me," he said.[105]

Just then the officer came and said, "Boys, the train is due soon. Get ready." When we were ready he took out some handcuffs and tied us together and we went to the station. The white people looked at us in surprise and called out our names and asked what the trouble was. Then the train arrived and we boarded it. We rode all that night and arrived in the morning. Then the officer locked us up in prison. We did not know what to say. After a time I was taken out and brought to the court house. There they again questioned me. A woman was there; a shorthand writer. Then he told me to tell again in detail (what I had told him), and that as soon as the time for the trial arrived he would let me return home. I therefore again told them where we had done the deed and the place; all this I told them in detail. Then when I was through he locked me up again. Then they took the other man to the court. When he returned he had (of course) learned what I had done. He was very quiet. Then I said, "Well, you said you were asked to kill him and you also said that you asked others to kill him. If that is so, you did it because you were asked to do so and you are not to blame.[106] If there are witnesses (to this fact), we will get out," I said. "And then again I said this because they had locked us up alone. I did not like it. The boys were so boisterous; the others ought to be in jail too. That is what I was thinking of when I said it. (Soon) they will bring

---

105 No better proof of S. B.'s honesty in this autobiography could be demanded than this very damaging evidence he gives against himself.

His attempt to justify his deed by claiming that the murdered man's brothers hated him and had actually asked him (Peter) to kill him, seems amusing to us. Personally, I feel that something more is involved here than a clumsy attempt at self-justification. To the Winnebago, words have a more definite meaning than to us and if the murdered man's brothers did actually express their hatred openly and ask someone to kill him, if, indeed, only such a wish on their part was known among the people, S. B. is merely giving expression to the normal Winnebago viewpoint, in claiming here and in another passage farther on that these brothers shared in the guilt of slaying this man.

106 He clearly intimates that since he (Peter) was asked to kill this man by the man's own brothers he is free from guilt. The only question, therefore, is to prove it. I do not think that S. B. is merely insisting upon witnesses because such is the white man's procedure. We are dealing here with a war-exploit and that was practically the only case where the Winnebago often refused to believe one another unless they took an oath. It is possible that the testimony of witnesses was also accepted.

the boys back and when there are a number of us here, it will not be so lonesome.[107]   He was glad of it.   After a while the others were brought.   There were now four of us.   We would make a good deal of noise talking.

25. THE CHARACTER OF THE MURDERED POTTAWATTOMIE

About that time it was reported that the man to whom we had done this had been rather crazy.   There were three brothers and the one we (killed) did this to, was the oldest.   Their father had been a chief and they had possessed much land.   The others had contributed much money to buy the land.   A number of them lived there and they had put in many crops.   Then the father of these three men died, and he (the oldest) drove the other people away.   When their parent died, he (the oldest) drove these people and his brothers away, it is said.   They had many horses and he forcibly kept all these things, it was said.   When he heard that any of his brothers were using the horses, he scolded them.   When they argued with him, he threatened to shoot them.   It was said that he always went around with his gun.   For all these reasons his brothers disliked him, it is said, and used to ask Winnebago to kill him.   It was also said that all his white neighbors disliked him.   He had over a hundred horses and they grew wild in the woods.   He did nothing all the time but watch them.[108]   He was not able to get near any of them;[109] the only use he ever made of them was to own them.   Whenever the horses entered a field, they would destroy it completely and if anything was ever said

---

[107] That he dreaded lonesomeness is probably true.   The true reason he has given us above, and this was only an excuse invented on the spur of the moment.   The statement that Peter was pleased at the idea of having company is unquestionably true.

[108] It is regarded as a sign of stinginess to watch one's possessions all the time.

[109] To be stingy and not even make use of one's possessions personally was regarded as both stupid and inimical to the common good.   Horses that were not being used belonged to anyone who cared to use them.   A man did not lose the ownership of an object by not using it, but the person who was using it obtained a kind of squatter's right to it.   At least such was the average Winnebago's view, not always admitted, however, by the owner.   The same point came out in connection with the war-bundle of the thunder-bird clan which was the personal property of S. B.'s brother who had inherited it from his father.   When he became a member of the peyote religion he wished to sell it to me, but the people who were at the time using it claimed that he had no right to it any longer because he was not making any use of it and they were.   He insisted on his proprietary rights but failed to get the war-bundle because popular opinion, at least, was on the side of those who were using it.   My impression was, however, that no one believed that he had permanently lost his proprietary rights in the bundle and that had he returned to the old tribal practices it would have been immediately returned to him without grumbling.

to him he immediately wanted to fight those (who complained). Whenever a person tried to buy one from him, he used to ask an extravagant price,[110] and if one of these (horses) was occasionally taken and he was asked to pay damages, he would threaten to shoot these people. He would go around barefooted with his gun, it was said. For all these reasons his brothers disliked him, and asked the Winnebago to shoot him. They told in what way it was possible to kill him,[111] and then asked someone to kill him, it was said. It was said that he belonged to that class of men whom it was impossible to kill. When he fasted he went without food for a whole winter, until spring, it was said.[112] To kill him one would have to have a wooden knife, paint it red and then stab him with it. Only thus could he be killed, it was said. With all this (evidence) the boys thought we would surely be acquitted.[113]

26. OUR PRISON–LIFE AND THE TRIAL

We were waiting for the spring term of the court. We stayed there all winter. I was very tired of it but I kept that secret, because we used to tease one another.[114] Sometimes I would feel like crying, but I would act as though I did not care at all. I was married at that time and I longed to see my wife and was terribly wrought up, but I told the others that I did not care in the least. The others

---

[110] Not only unjustifiable but unfair and unethical.

[111] As indicated farther on it was believed that he could only be killed in a certain way. The Pottawattomie were regarded by the Winnebago as possessing uncommon shamanistic powers.

[112] The most powerful blessings were obtained by those who had the strength to fast for so long a period.

[113] i.e., by showing first that he was a wicked man, a nuisance to the community, and that even his own brothers had desired his death. It must also be remembered that S. B. brought Winnebago notions of punishment into this whole question and that while he could see how the Whites might regard the killing of a hereditary enemy as murder, yet he probably expected them to demand the same amends that his own tribesmen would have demanded, namely a payment of some kind to the relatives of the murdered man.

[114] There are two reasons why a Winnebago tries not to exhibit his emotions: first, because it is a sign of effeminacy, and secondly, because he thereby lays himself open to ridicule, playful or otherwise, which he dreads. The charge of effeminacy is only associated with the exhibition of suffering in connection with wounds received on the warpath, while being tortured, etc. In the instance cited by S. B. it is not the charge of effeminacy he fears but the possibility of being ridiculed. This apparently wounds a Winnebago's *amour propre* more than anything else and he is apt to remember it for long periods of time. I remember once seeing a chair break under the weight of a Winnebago, the laughter which followed, and the sheepish and angry face of the unfortunate man. Three years after that I happened to meet the same Indian again. He did not at first recognize me but remembered me as soon as I recalled the incident to him. He told me then with glee how he had only recently been revenged on one of those who laughed so heartily at his mishap by playing some practical joke on him.

were also married and some of them showed their lonesomeness markedly. Sometimes one of the women would visit us and the others always said that I was the only one who did not seem to care. (As a matter of fact), I could hardly stand it, but I kept my condition quite secret. I only felt better when I wrote a letter to my wife, and when she wrote to me I felt very happy.

We used to read one another's letters. Whenever our wives wrote to us we would tease one another about the things that were said in these letters.

After a while the spring term of the court arrived and we were happy. However, when the time for the trial came, we were bound over to the fall term. So we stayed there all summer. Then the fall term came and we were bound over until the next spring term. It was enough to cause one to say, O my! (in impatience). During the winter we made bead work. We used to compete to see who could do the best work. We used to make beaded finger rings and they were always purchased from us. After a while we had a good deal of money, for we would sell many rings. After a while we made some suspenders. I made thirty of them and we used to sell these for seven dollars a pair. We thus always had plenty of money and we always drank. Some of the people locked up in prison with us, whose terms were almost over, would be allowed to go outside and these would buy us whiskey. We also used to gamble with one another. We would play for money.

One day my wife came to visit me. I talked with her through the iron grating. They allowed me to talk to her for a long time. All I could do was to desire her. I wanted her badly. When the wives of the others came they felt just as I did.

Once we had a fight. We had been drinking and were disputing about a game. Afterwards we were quite humble about it.

Some time after this, we found out that my wife had married again. I did not feel like eating, but I tried hard to do so, because I thought that the others would notice it.[115]   Then I said, "I am glad to hear that it is reported that my wife has married again. When I get out of prison, I will pay the one who has (married her), for he is going to take care of her until I get out. I had been quite uneasy about her for some time, and now I feel quite relieved, for

---

[115] Cf. note 114. Realizing that he would not be able to hide his condition, he prefers to tell his companions in a grandiloquent way that a load has been taken off his mind, in order thus to escape the bantering that was bound to take place.

she is going to be taken care of.'' Thus I said. But the truth of it was that I was about as angry as I could be. I made up my mind that I would take her away from whomsoever she might be living with. Then I thought I would make her feel as sad as I could. I thought that I would disfigure her[116] and leave her; or take her away in the wilderness, whip her soundly, and then leave her there. I could not think of anything else and I did not even know how the food tasted. I often felt like crying. At night I would not be able to sleep, for I could not forget it. I would try to dream of her when I went to sleep at night. Sometimes I would dream of seeing her and then in the morning I would tell the others about it and I would feel better. I never thought of any of my relatives who were really the ones who felt deeply for me.[117] I was not even that (grateful). I only thought of the woman.

The time for the next court term had arrived, and we were taken over to the court. It was the spring term. We were given a trial. When we were taken to the court, they would always handcuff two of us together. We each had a lawyer. At our first hearing, one of us was freed, and three remained in prison. Then the lawyers pleaded our case and two more of us were freed. The one who had actually done the killing was the only one who remained in prison.[118]

27. MY RELEASE FROM PRISON

When we got out, we found our relatives waiting for us. My elder brother was there and I went home with him. We began to drink immediately. I was very happy,[119] although when I was in prison I had felt that I would never drink again.

That same day we reached the Winnebago. There I saw a woman whom I married that very night. I had been desiring women for a long time. Then I began to drink again. Then I went on to Black River Falls and when I got there I saw my former wife and I took her back again.

---

[116] i.e., punish her as an adulteress used to be punished by the Winnebago, by cutting off her nose.

[117] Whatever remorse he ever expresses is for his relatives, as is to be expected considering the intensity of the family tie.

[118] This must probably have appeared to S. B. and the Winnebago in general as an amusing indication of the white man's incurable ignorance, for the man who actually kills the enemy is regarded as only second in importance to the four who count coup. That these three should have been acquitted and the other person imprisoned was the height of the ridiculous.

[119] No attempt is ever made to hide the expression of joy except when strangers are around.

The Indians were celebrating their midsummer ceremony. I went there and took part and I drank all the time. I considered myself a brave man and a medicine man and I also thought myself a holy man, a strong man, and a favorite with women.[120] I regarded myself as being in possession of many courting medicines. I am a great man, I thought, and also a fleet runner. I was a good singer of Brave Dance songs.[121] I was a sport and I wanted whiskey every day.

My mother and father had gone to Missouri River (Winnebago reservation in Nebraska) and left me in charge of the two horses they possessed, as well as a vehicle which I was using at the time. Later on, in the fall, when the cranberry season started, I lived with three women. I never did any work, but simply went from one of these women to the other. After a while an annuity payment was made. I went around ''chasing the payments'' and I sold the horses at that time and spent the money.

28. MY FIRST ACQUAINTANCE WITH THE PEYOTE

Then my father and mother asked me to come to the Missouri River (Nebraska) but I had been told that my father and mother had eaten peyote[122] and I did not like it. I had been told that these peyote eaters were doing wrong, and therefore I disliked them;[123] I had heard that they were doing everything that was wicked. For these reasons we did not like them. About this time they sent me money for my ticket and since my brothers and sisters told me to go, I went. Just as I was about to start, my youngest sister, the one to whom we always listened most attentively, said to me, ''Older brother, do not you indulge in this medicine eating (Peyote) of which so much is said.'' I promised. Then I started out.

---

[120] The ideal of every Winnebago man.

[121] Songs sung at the *Herucka* dance.

[122] For details of this cult cf. my article ''The Peyote Cult of the Winnebago,'' Jour. Relig. Psych., VII, pp. 1–22, and the article ''peyote'' in Hastings' ''Encyclopaedia of Religion and Ethics.'' His conservative relatives were quick to recognize what danger he would run of being converted if he stayed with his parents. Events subsequently proved how correct was their fear.

[123] The feeling against the peyote-eaters was very intense, not because they had introduced a new cult or because there were Christian elements in this cult, but because the peyote followers insisted that all the other ceremonies were wrong and must be abandoned and because they destroyed war-bundles, medicine-bags, etc., everything dear to the hearts of the conservative Winnebago. S. B. here shows clearly that in spite of the many strictures he makes concerning his religious feeling, he was apparently just as religious as the average Winnebago.

As soon as I arrived (in Nebraska) I met some people who had not joined the peyote eaters[124] and who said to me, "Your relatives are eating the peyote and they sent for you that you also might eat it. Your mother, your father, and your younger sister, they are all eating it." Thus they spoke to me. Then they told me of some of the bad things it was reported that these people had done. I felt ashamed and I wished I had not come in the first place. Then I said that I was going to eat the medicine.[125]

After that I saw my father, mother, and sister. They were glad. Then we all went to where they were staying. My father and I walked (alone). Then he told me about the peyote eating. "It does not amount to anything, all this that they are doing, although they do stop drinking.[126] It is also said that sick people get well. We were told about this and so we joined, and, sure enough, we are practically well, your mother as well as I. It is said that they offer prayers to Earthmaker (God)," he said. He kept on talking. "They are rather foolish. They cry when they feel very happy about anything. They throw away all of the medicines that they possess and know. They give up all the blessings they received while fasting and they give up all the spirits that blessed them in their fasts. They also stop smoking and chewing tobacco. They stop giving feasts, and they stop making offerings of tobacco. Indeed they burn up their holy things. They burn up their war-bundles. They are bad people. They give up the Medicine Dance. They burn up their medicine bags and even cut up their otter-skin bags. They say they are praying to Earthmaker (God) and they do so standing and crying. They claim that they

---

124 The drift toward the peyote cult about this time, 1907, was very great in Nebraska and the conservatives were frightened at the inroads the new faith was making even among the members of their most conservative and popular ceremony, the Medicine Dance. Every newcomer was immediately warned against the degrading effects of eating the peyote. The peyote people, on the contrary, carried on no open campaign but resorted to the far more insidious and effective method of winning new people to their cult by treating them with kindness and consideration.

125 It was clearly foolish for the conservatives and strangers to insist upon the evil effects of peyote while at the same time informing S. B. that his parents and his younger sister belonged to the sect, for family pride was bound to assert itself. Thus I understand S. B.'s sudden declaration that he was going to eat the peyote. It was tantamount to telling them to mind their own business. He had then, of course, no intention of doing anything of the kind.

126 So completely did all those who joined the peyote cult give up drinking that many Indians and whites were at first inclined to believe that this was a direct effect of the peyote. However this is an error. The correct explanation is that John Rave, the leader of the cult, gave up drinking when he became a convert and included this renunciation of all liquors in the cult which he so largely moulded and dominated. If any additional proof were needed it can be found in the fact that as Rave's personal influence decreased and as the membership increased the number of people who drank liquor and ate peyote at the same time increased.

hold nothing holy except Earthmaker (God). They claim that all the things that they are stopping are those of the bad spirit (the devil), and that the bad spirit (the devil) has deceived them; that there are no spirits who can bless; that there is no other spirit except Earthmaker (God)." Then I said, "Say, they certainly speak foolishly."[127] I felt very angry towards them. "You will hear them for they are going to have a meeting tonight. Their songs are very strange. They use a very small drum," said he. Then I felt a very strong desire to see them.[128]

After a while we arrived. At night they had their ceremony. At first I sat outside and listened to them. I was rather fond of them. I stayed in that country and the young peyote eaters were exceedingly friendly to me. They would give me a little money now and then and they treated me with tender regard. They did everything that they thought would make me feel good, and in consequence I used to speak as though I liked their ceremony. However I was only deceiving them. I only said it, because they were so good to me. I thought they acted in this way because (the peyote) was deceiving them.

Soon after that my parents returned to Wisconsin, but when they left they said they would come back in a little while. So I was left there with my relatives who were all peyote followers. For that reason they left me there. Whenever I went among the non-peyote people I used to say all sorts of things about the peyote people and when I returned to the peyote people, I used to say all sorts of things about the others.

I had a friend who was a peyote man and he said to me, "My friend, I wish very much that you should eat the peyote." Thus he spoke and I answered him, "My friend, I will do it, but not until I get accustomed to the people of this country.[129] Then I will do it.

---

[127] This rather remarkable speech of S. B.'s father is of course designed to get his son interested, and in this he succeeds admirably. His frequent declarations that the peyote cult was of no consequence is to be interpreted in two ways: first, in order not to antagonize too much his son who is, after all, still a conservative, and secondly as a survival of what might be called "ritualistic" modesty. In all speeches delivered at ceremonies it was customary to depreciate one's self and one's powers. It is this last tendency which I am inclined to see here, although in his case derogatory remarks are also made about the ceremony itself and other participants in the ceremony, an element entirely absent from the speeches found in the older rituals.

[128] The speech has had the desired effect and the last touch, appealing to every Winnebago's desire for novelty, has been particularly effective.

[129] There are a number of differences between the Wisconsin and the Nebraska divisions of the tribe, but nothing to justify this statement. While this is merely an excuse, his other declaration as to his being worried about the ridicule to which the peyote people were being subjected is quite truthful, although he claims this too to be merely an excuse.

The only thing that worries me is the fact that they are making fun of you. And in addition, I am not quite used to them." I spoke dishonestly.

I was staying at the place where my sister lived. She had gone to Oklahoma; she was a peyote follower. After a while she returned. I was then living with a number of women. This was the second time (there) and from them I obtained some money. Once I got drunk there and was locked up for six days. After my sister returned she and the others paid more attention than ever to me. Especially was this true of my brother-in-law. They gave me horses and a vehicle. They really treated me very tenderly. I knew that they did all this because they wished me to eat the peyote.[130] I, in my turn, was very kind to them. I thought that I was fooling them and they thought that they were converting me.[131] I told them that I believed in the peyote because they were treating me so nicely.

After a while we moved to a certain place where they were to have a large peyote meeting. I knew they were doing this in order to get me to join.[132] Then I said to my younger sister, "I would be quite willing to eat this peyote (ordinarily), but I don't like the woman with whom I am living just now and I think I will leave her. That is why I do not want to join now, for I understand that when married people eat medicine (peyote) they will always have to stay together. Therefore I will join when I am married to some woman permanently." Then my brother-in-law came and she told him what I had said, and he said to me, "You are right in what you say. The woman with whom you are staying is a married woman and you can not continue living with her. It is null and void (this marriage) and we know it.[133] You had better join now. It will be the same as if

---

130 Their motives were mixed. They seem to have had all the characteristics of the early Christian proselytizers.

131 He is probably wrong, both in his interpretation of his own motives and of theirs. No Winnebago accepts favors and acts of kindness from others without feeling a sense of obligation. In a way, he is giving us here the interpretation of the conservatives.

132 He is quite right. It is exceedingly interesting to note how insidious the methods of his peyote relatives have been. Not a word have they said to him about the ceremony, with the exception of his father's rather negative speech. But they, his relatives, have piled kindness upon kindness and this too after his release from prison, and after an absence of many months. They have so thoroughly enmeshed him in obligations that they feel they can take the risk of bringing him to a performance of the ceremony, while he, overwhelmed by the sense of obligation, is now concerned merely with putting them off as long as he can, with any pretext he can find.

133 His rather clever excuse is immediately parried by his brother-in-law with the Christian conception of marriage.

you were single.[134] We will pray for you as though you were single.
After you have joined this ceremony, then you can marry any woman
whom you have a right to marry (legally). So, do join tonight. It
is best. For some time we have been desirous of your joining but
we have not said anything to you.[135] It is Earthmaker's (God's)
blessing to you that you have been thinking of this,''[136] said he.

29. I EAT PEYOTE

Therefore I sat inside the meeting-place with them. One man
acted as leader. We were to do whatever he ordered. The regalia
were placed before him.[137] I wanted to sit in some place on the side,
because I thought I might get to crying like the others. I felt ashamed
of myself.[138]

Then the leader arose and talked. He said that this was an affair
of Earthmaker's (God's), and that he (the leader) could do nothing
on his own initiative; that Earthmaker (God) was going to conduct
the ceremony. Then he said that the medicine (peyote) was holy
and that he would turn us all over to it;[139] that he had turned himself
over to it and wished now to turn all of us over to it. He said further,
''I am a very pitiable (figure) in this ceremony,[140] so when you pray
to Earthmaker, pray also for me. Now let us all rise and pray to
Earthmaker (God).'' We all rose. Then he prayed. He prayed
for the sick, and he prayed for those who did not yet know Earth-

---

[134] Apparently he considers the opportunity too favorable to let pass. S. B.
must join immediately.

[135] Now that S. B. has taken the initiative there is no longer any danger in
informing him that they desired him to join the cult.

[136] It is difficult to determine whether this is merely a Christian interpretation
or an old Winnebago concept. S. B.'s father very definitely expresses the same
viewpoint in connection with S. B.'s war exploit when he says that S. B. could not
have thought of it (his undertaking against the Pottawattomie) at his own suggestion, but that the spirits had suggested it. Cf. note 89.

[137] Consisting of two peyote, one considered female, one male; a drum, an
eagle wing fan, and a small gourd rattle. These regalia and the custom of placing
them in front of the leader who then passes them on, are ideas taken over directly
from the older ceremonies.   .

[138] After midnight when the effect of the peyote is beginning to manifest
itself, it is customary for certain members, any who desire, to go up to the leader
and there make a confession of their sins, during which time they cry profusely.
This is what he is referring to. Strong remorse, even among the older people,
was frequently accompanied by crying.

[139] A phrase borrowed from Christianity, which has become a ritualistic
formula, meaning that they were going to enter into communion with Earthmaker
through the mediation of the peyote.

[140] Here again the new and the old religious ideas mingle. The phrase itself
is a verbatim introduction to the regular speeches delivered at any ceremony, yet,
at the same time, he unquestionably wishes to imply that God alone presides over
their meeting and that the suppliants should offer their prayers directly to him.
This is a Christian and an imported notion.

maker.[141] He said that they were to be pitied. When he had finished
we sat down. Then the peyote was passed around. They gave me
five. My brother-in-law said to me, "If you speak to this medicine
(peyote), it will give you whatever you ask of it.[142] Then you must
pray to Earthmaker, and then you must eat the medicine." However
I ate them (the peyote) immediately for I did not know what to ask
for and I did not know what to say in a prayer to Earthmaker (God).
So I ate the peyote just as they were.[143] They were very bitter and
had a taste difficult to describe. I wondered what would happen to
me. After a while I was given five more and I also ate them. They
tasted rather bitter. Now I was very quiet. The peyote rather weak-
ened me. Then I listened very attentively to the singing. I liked it
very much.[144] I felt as though I were partly asleep. I felt different
from (my normal self), but when I (looked around) and examined
myself, I saw nothing wrong about myself. However I felt different
from (my normal self). Before this I used to dislike the songs. Now
I liked the leader's singing very much. I liked to listen to him.

They were all sitting very quietly. They were doing nothing
except singing. Each man sang four songs and then passed the regalia
to the next one. (Each one) held a stick and an eagle's tail feather in
one hand and a small gourd rattle, which they used to shake while
singing, in the other. One of (those) present used to do the drumming. Thus objects would pass around until they came back to the
leader, who would then sing four songs. When these were finished,
he would place the various (things) on the ground,[145] rise, and pray
to Earthmaker (God). Then he called upon one or two to speak.
They said that Earthmaker (God) was good and that the peyote was
good, and that whosoever ate this medicine (peyote) would be able
to free himself from the bad spirit (the devil) ; for they said that
Earthmaker forbids us to commit sins. When this was over they
sang again.

---

[141] This is of distinctly Christian origin.

[142] This is, of course, good Winnebago doctrine. The peyote was in other
words to be treated as a medicinal herb. One of the essential elements of the
older culture, namely, the offering of tobacco, is, however, absent.

It might be added that this conception of the peyote and its powers, although
it was that of the leader and the older members of the cult, was not shared by
the younger adherents who had come into more intimate contact with Christianity
and some of whom could read the Bible. At least this was the case in 1908–1909.
Since then, however, I understand that the older, original, conception has been
adopted by the majority.

[143] The peyote are either eaten in their dried condition or taken in a liquid
concoction.

[144] Here again we have S. B. in an expectant mood. He is waiting, as in his
former fasts, for some inward change.

[145] This is exactly the procedure in the old pagan ceremonies.

After midnight, every once in a while, (I heard) someone cry. In some cases they would go up to the leader and talk with him. He would stand up and pray with them. They told me what they were saying. They said that they were asking (people) to pray for them, as they were sorry for their sins and that they might be prevented from committing them again. That is what they were saying. They cried very loudly. I was rather frightened. (I noticed also) that when I closed my eyes and sat still, I began to see strange things. I did not get sleepy in the least. Thus the light (of morning) came upon me. In the morning, as the sun rose, they stopped.[146] They all got up and prayed to Earthmaker (God) and then they stopped.

During the daytime, I did not get sleepy in the least. My actions were a little different (from my usual ones). Then they said, "To-night they are going to have another meeting. Let us go over. They say that is the best (thing) to do and thus you can learn it (the ceremony) right away. It is said that their spirits wander over all the earth and the heavens also. All this you will learn and see," they said.[147] "At times they die[148] and remain dead all night and all day. When in this condition they sometimes see Earthmaker (God),[149] it is said." One would also be able to see where the bad spirit lived, it was said.

---

[146] Exactly as they stop at this time in the pagan ceremonies.

[147] The notion itself is typical of the Winnebago. Such powers, however, were obtained in former times not by membership in a ceremony but through blessings from spirits. The phraseology is markedly reminiscent of the descriptions of the old Winnebago spirits. It is interesting to note that while in former times this power was desired for some purpose, here all that an individual is to receive is the power itself.

[148] i.e., become unconscious and have visions. The notion itself is old. That is what was expected during fasting except that the semi-delirious condition of the faster was never spoken of as dying. This notion probably arose from the observation of a number of cases of complete prostration due to an overdose of peyote; and of cataleptic fits. I think it may even have been due to the cataleptic fits of one of the leaders, A. H., which were well-known and frequently commented upon. He himself was in the habit of describing at great length what he saw during these seizures. However, the starting point may also have been the death and resurrection enacted in the Medicine Dance or the holy condition which certain fasters and certain exceptional participants in ceremonies brought upon themselves.
The visions in these cases were always superinduced by the peyote.

[149] The leader mentioned in note 148 claimed to have seen and spoken to God. However, this was an old Winnebago notion. A number of people had tried in their fasting to see Earthmaker, with whom God is now equated. There is, as a matter of fact, a story about one of S. B.'s ancestors who partially succeeded in seeing Eathmaker. This I have published in "The Autobiography of a Winnebago Indian," Jour. American Folk-Lore, vol. xxvi, no. cii, 1913. A. H.'s vision of God was generally known and all new converts tried to emulate him. Visits to Earthmaker and the evil spirit (Herecgu'nina) are frequently mentioned in the old myths.

So we went there again. I doubted all this. I thought that what they were saying was untrue.[150] However I went along anyhow. When we got there I had already eaten some peyote, for I had taken three during the day. Now near the peyote meeting an (Indian) feast was being given and I went there instead. When I reached the place, I saw a long lodge. The noise was terrific. They were beating an enormous drum. The sound almost raised me in the air, so (pleasurably) loud did it sound to me.[151] Not so (pleasurable) had things appeared at those affairs (peyote meetings) that I had lately been attending. There I danced all night and I flirted with the women. About day I left and when I got back the peyote meeting was still going on. When I got back they told me to sit down at a certain place. They treated me very kindly. There I again ate peyote. I heard that they were going to have another meeting nearby on the evening of the same day. We continued eating peyote the whole day at the place where we were staying.[152] We were staying at the house of one of my relatives. Some of the boys there taught me a few songs. "Say, when you learn how to sing, you will be the best singer, for you are a good singer as it is. You have a good voice," they said to me. I thought so myself.

30. THE EFFECTS OF THE PEYOTE

That night we went to the place where the peyote meeting was to take place. They gave me a place to sit and treated me very kindly. "Well, he has come," they even said when I got there, "make a place for him." I thought they regarded me as a great man. John Rave,[153]

---

[150] True to his refusal to believe anything of a religious nature unless he should experience some inward change, he still considers everything that he has so far seen and heard, untrue.

[151] He here voices his delight at getting away from the rather ethical and puritanical atmosphere of the peyote people and again participating in the rites dear to him. The phraseology he uses is the customary one to express the superlative degree of happiness. It is always used to describe the dances indulged in by the ghosts of the departed in spirit-land, who are the happiest of people. This reads almost like a verbatim quotation from the description of the life spirits lead as pictured in the very popular "Origin Myth of the Four Nights' Wake."

[152] It was quite customary to eat peyote during the day in the early days of the peyote cult.

[153] A very remarkable man, the leader and directing power of the peyote religion. He became a convert to it in Oklahoma and introduced his version of the cult among the Winnebago. A powerful personality and a wonderful organizer, he moulded the cult he had borrowed into something quite new. He possessed the proselytizing zeal to an unusual degree. Through his activity the Winnebago form of the peyote cult has been spread among the Fox, Menominee, Ojibwa, and Dakota.

the leader, was to conduct the (ceremony). I ate five peyote. Then my brother-in-law and my sister came and gave themselves up.[154] They asked me to stand there with them. I did not like it, but I did it nevertheless. "Why should I give myself up? I am not in earnest, and I intend to stop this as soon as I get back to Wisconsin. I am only doing this because they have given me presents," I thought. "I might just as well get up, since it doesn't mean anything to me." So I stood up. The leader began to talk and I (suddenly) began to feel sick. It got worse and worse and finally I lost consciousness entirely.[155] When I recovered I was lying flat on my back. Those with whom I had been standing, were still standing there. I had (as a matter of fact) regained consciousness as soon as I fell down. I felt like leaving the place that night, but I did not do it.[156] I was quite tired out. "Why have I done this?" I said to myself. "I promised (my sister) that I would not do it." So I thought and then I tried to leave, but I could not. I suffered intensely.[157] At last daylight came upon me. Now I thought that they regarded me as one who had had a trance and found out something.[158]

Then we went home and they showed me a passage in the Bible where it said that it was a shame for any man to wear long hair.[159] That is what it said, they told me. I looked at the passage. I was not a man learned in books, but I wanted to give the impression that I knew how to read, so I told them to cut my hair, for I wore it long at that time. After my hair was cut I took out a lot of medicine that I happened to have in my pockets. These were courting medicines.

[154] The actual rite of giving one's self up consisted in standing before the leader who preached to them and together with them offered up prayers. It was generally a very dramatic moment.

[155] Apparently the effect of the large number of peyote he had eaten.

[156] One of the most marked effects of eating peyote is a feeling of extreme weariness.

[157] Peyote is supposed to have a very disagreeable effect upon some individuals. This feeling, however, passes away after a while. One of the commonest effects is a feeling of strangulation and general impotence. This suffering, so individuals told me, increases if one struggles against it. Rave, very early after his conversion, interpreted these effects of the peyote as symbolizing the struggle between the peyote and the particular vices of an individual. The increase in the intensity of his suffering when resistance was offered, corresponded to his unwillingness to give up the old life.

[158] He is, of course, still unconverted and has come to the same conclusion at which he had arrived during his unsuccessful fasting experiences. Having gone through the ceremony, however, and having actually become unconscious, he was quite willing to let them imagine that he had seen what they had told him he would see. Such had been his procedure throughout life.

[159] This was part of their campaign against the old customs and habits; one of the characteristics introduced by A. H., who knew the Bible fairly well and whose influence was then at its height, especially among the younger people.

There were many small bundles of them. All these, together with my hair, I gave to my brother-in-law. Then I cried and my brother-in-law also cried. Then he thanked me. He told me that I understood and that I had done well.[160] He told me that Earthmaker (God) alone was holy; that all the things (blessings and medicines) that I possessed, were false; that I had been fooled by the bad spirit (devil). He told me that I had now freed myself from much of this (bad influence). My relatives expressed their thanks fervently.

On the fourth night they had another meeting and I went to it again. There I again ate (peyote). I enjoyed it and I sang along with them. I wanted to be able to sing immediately. Some young men were singing and I enjoyed it, so I prayed to Earthmaker asking him to let me learn to sing right away.[161] That was all I asked for. My brother-in-law was with me all the time. At that meeting all the things I had given my brother-in-law were burned up.

The fact that he (my brother-in-law) told me that I understood, pleased me, and I felt good when daylight came. (As a matter of fact) I had not received any knowledge.[162] However I thought it was the proper way to act, so I did it.

After that I would attend meetings every once in a while and I looked around for a woman whom I might marry permanently. Before long that was the only thing I thought of when I attended the meetings.

31. I AM CONVERTED

On one occasion we were to have a meeting of men and I went to the meeting with a woman, with whom I thought of going around the next day. That was (the only) reason I went with her.[163] When we arrived, the one who was to lead, asked me to sit near him. There he placed me. He urged me to eat a lot of peyote, so I did. The leaders (of the ceremony) always place the regalia in front of them-

---

[160] He had, externally at least, become a member of the cult. It is extremely interesting to note how they accept his conversion merely because he has permitted his hair to be cut and has given up his *medicines,* for this is simply the old Winnebago attitude. Of course he is almost on the verge of conversion, even from his own standpoint, as is evidenced by his crying.

[161] In a former passage when he had been told to pray to God he did not know what to ask for, but now that there is something definite he wishes to possess he finds no difficulty in praying. This he understood; the other, more general prayer, he did not.

[162] i.e., he has not yet experienced the inward change upon which he insists.

[163] Apparently he feels that the motive is wrong now that he is a member of the peyote cult.

selves; they also had a peyote placed there.[164]   The one this leader
placed in front of himself this time, was a very small one.   "Why
does he have a very small one there?" I thought to myself. I did not
think much about it.

It was now late at night and I had eaten a lot of peyote and felt
rather tired. I suffered considerably. After a while I looked at the
peyote and there stood an eagle with outspread wings. It was as
beautiful a sight as one could behold. Each of the feathers seemed
to have a mark. The eagle stood looking at me. I looked around
thinking that perhaps there was something the matter with my sight.
Then I looked again and it was really there. I then looked in a
different direction and it disappeared. Only the small peyote remained.[165]   I looked around at the other people but they all had
their heads bowed and were singing. I was very much surprised.

Some time after this (I saw) a lion lying in the same place (where
I had seen the eagle). I watched it very closely. It was alive and
looking at me. I looked at it very closely and when I turned my
eyes away just the least little bit, it disappeared. "I suppose they
all know this and I am just beginning to know of it," I thought.
Then I saw a small person (at the same place). He wore blue clothes
and a shining brimmed cap. He had on a soldier's uniform.[166]   He
was sitting on the arm of the person who was drumming, and he
looked at every one. He was a little man, perfect (in all propor-
tions). Finally I lost sight of him. I was very much surprised
indeed. I sat very quietly. "This is what it is," I thought, "this
is what they all probably see and I am just beginning to find out."

Then I prayed to Earthmaker (God): *"This, your ceremony, let
me hereafter perform."*[167]

---

[164] The largest and most perfect peyote they happen to possess which they call
huñk', chief, as a rule, set aside for this purpose.

[165] He apparently had one of the gorgeous color visions which are frequently
induced by eating peyote. Whether we are to interpret the fact that he saw an
eagle as connected with blessings from eagle spirits, it is difficult to say.

[166] This is one of the customary visions seen in fasts. Such a spirit appeared
to S. B.'s brother when he was fasting. This unquestioned reminiscence of the
old fasting experiences suggests that in the two former visions he was also
influenced by the old conceptions. We see here the same kind of degeneration
as that pointed out in note 140. The figures (spirits) appear, but they have no
function; they have become devitalized.

[167] These three visions apparently gave him that sense of an inward change
for which he had looked in vain during his early fasts. The italicized sentences
are identical with the words used by John Rave in the account of his conversion,
and I imagine that his words became a kind of formula used by many people
in describing the actual moment of conversion.

32. I SEE EARTHMAKER (GOD) AND HAVE OTHER VISIONS

As I looked again, I saw a flag. I looked more carefully and (I saw) the house full of flags. They had the most beautiful marks on them. In the middle (of the room) there was a very large flag and it was a live one; it was moving. In the doorway there was another one not entirely visible. I had never seen anything so beautiful in all my life before.[168]

Then again I prayed to Earthmaker (God). I bowed my head and closed my eyes and began (to speak).[169] I said many things that I would ordinarily never has spoken about.[170] As I prayed, I was aware of something above me and there he was; Earthmaker (God) to whom I was praying, he it was.[171] That which is called the soul, that is it, that is what one calls Earthmaker (God).[172] Now this is what I felt and saw. The one called Earthmaker (God) is a spirit and that is what I felt and saw. All of us sitting there, we had all together one spirit or soul; at least that is what I learned. I instantly became the spirit and I was their spirit or soul. Whatever they thought of, I (immediately) knew it.[173] I did not have to speak to them and get an answer to know what their thoughts had

---

[168] This, as well as the spread wings of the eagle, is clearly a color vision.

[169] The bowing of the head and the closing of the eyes are old Winnebago customs. It is the fact that the peyote worshippers pray standing that is new.

[170] Apparently both a prayer and a confession. It was the belief of the peyote followers that a new convert would not feel at ease until he had made a complete admission of the error of his former life. Some even believed that the cardinal vices would be symbolically vomited by the new adherent. One individual told me that he felt, at conversion, as though he had vomited a bulldog, which he explained as representing his former pugnacity and stubbornness.

[171] His vision of Earthmaker is more like the old visions of spirits and is quite different from A. H.'s visions of God. The latter's were distinctly Christian in origin and he had them only during a cataleptic fit. S. B. has Earthmaker appear to him in very much the same manner that certain spirits were supposed to manifest themselves to the Winnebago in former times. Certain spirits were never seen but were recognized by the rustling of the wind, leaves, etc.; while the presence of others was merely felt as he says here of Earthmaker. Earthmaker, as the apparitions mentioned before, is quite functionless. S. B. merely sees him. Cf. note 166.

[172] This is S. B.'s personal metaphysics and shows how completely he, at least, misunderstood what Rave and A. H. meant by their identification of Earthmaker with God. S. B. probably knew little and bothered himself less about the old concept of Earthmaker for he was not a priest. Knowing little of the older belief he was hard put to it, I imagine, when the new God was defined in terms of the old. Hence arose perhaps this unusual identification of God with soul. In his keyed-up condition of religious expectancy and fervor he apparently identified his sensations with this new God.

[173] This power of knowing beforehand what a person was thinking of is a good Winnebago belief and is one of the gifts promised all those who join the Medicine Dance. There it is considered merely a magical gift resulting from membership in that organization. S. B. very cleverly and acutely has this power flow from his predication of a corporate soul, with which his individual soul is temporarily identified.

been. Then I thought of a certain place, far away, and immediately I was there; I was my thought.[174]

I looked around and noticed how everything seemed about me, and when I opened my eyes I was myself in the body again. From this time on, I thought, thus I shall be. This is the way they are, and I am only just beginning to be that way. "All those that heed Earthmaker (God) must be thus," I thought. I would not need any more food," I thought, "for was I not my spirit? Nor would I have any more use of my body," I felt. "My corporeal affairs are over," I felt.

Then they stopped and left for it was just dawning. Then someone spoke to me. I did not answer for I thought they were just fooling and that they were all like myself, and that (therefore) it was unnecessary for me to talk to them. So when they spoke to me I only answered with a smile. "They are just saying this to me because (they realize) that I have just found out," I thought. That was why I did not answer. I did not speak to anyone until noon. Then I had to leave the house to perform one of nature's duties and someone followed me. It was my friend. He said, "My friend, what troubles you that makes you act as you do?" "Well, there's no need of your saying anything for you know it beforehand," I said.

Then I immediately got over my trance and again got into my (normal) condition so that he would have to speak to me before I knew his thoughts. I became like my former self.[175] It became necessary for me to speak to him.

33. FURTHER CONSEQUENCES OF MY CONVERSION

Then I spoke to him and said, "My friend, let us hitch up these horses and then I will go wherever you like, for you wish to speak to me and I also want to go around and talk to you." Thus I spoke to him. "If I were to tell you all that I have learned, I would never be able to stop at all, so much have I learned," I said to him. "However, I would enjoy telling some of it." "Good," said he. He liked

---

[174] The power of transporting one's self at will to a distant place is likewise an old Winnebago conception which members of the Medicine Dance were supposed to possess. In saying that he was his thought he is elaborating his previous identification of himself with the corporate soul. No unnecessary philosophical implications are to be thought of in this connection. Thought, feeling, etc., were regarded by the Winnebago as objective realities, or, to put it more correctly perhaps, as things that existed just as definitely as what was perceived directly through the senses.

[175] He recovered from his trance.

it (what I told him) very much. "That is what I am anxious to hear," said he. Then we went after the horses. We caught one of them, but we could not get the other. He got away from us and we could not find him. We hunted everywhere for the horse but could not discover where he had run to. Long afterwards we found it among the whites.[176]

Now since that time (of my conversion) no matter where I am I always think of this religion. I still remember it and I think I will remember it as long as I live. It is the only holy thing that I have been aware of in all my life.

After that whenever I heard of a peyote meeting, I went to it. However my thoughts were always fixed on women. "If I were married (legally) perhaps these thoughts will leave me," I thought. Whenever I went to a meeting now I tried to eat as many peyote as possible, for I was told that it was good to eat them. For that reason I ate them. As I sat there I would always pray to Earthmaker (God). Now these were my thoughts. If I were married, I thought as I sat there, I could then put all my thoughts on this ceremony.[177] I sat with my eyes closed and was very quiet.

Suddenly I saw something. This was tied up. The rope with which this object was tied up was long. The object itself was running around and around (in a circle). There was a pathway there in which it ought to go, but it was tied up and unable to get there. The road was an excellent one. Along its edge blue grass grew and on each side there grew many varieties of pretty flowers. Sweet-smelling flowers sprang up all along this road.[178] Far off in the distance appeared a bright light.[179] There a city was visible of a beauty indescribable by tongue. A cross was in full sight.[180] The object that was tied up would always fall just short of reaching the

---

[176] Apparently this unimportant episode had become so definitely associated in his mind with the fundamental changes that were taking place in him, that he remembered it in great detail.

[177] This is merely the old Winnebago formula of "religious concentration."

[178] These words are taken verbatim from the Winnebago description of the road to spirit-land.

[179] This is of course Christian, but it is clearly an assimilation to the description of Earthmaker's lodge as seen from a distance after one has crossed the four hills as depicted in the myth of the journey to spirit-land in the Medicine Dance; a myth which, of course, S. B. knew very well.

[180] While the idea of the cross here is probably Christian it might be pointed out that two lines crossing at right angles was also the old symbol of Earthmaker and was always painted on the buck-skin offered to him at the war-bundle feasts. This symbol is also identified, among the Winnebago, with the four cardinal points.

road. It seemed to lack sufficient strength to break loose (of what was holding it). (Near it) lay something which would have given it sufficient strength to break its fastenings, if it were only able to get hold of it.

I looked at what was so inextricably tied up and I saw that it was myself. I was forever thinking of women.[181] "This it is with which I was tied," I thought. "Were I married, I would have strength enough to break my fastening and be able to travel in the good road," I thought. Then daylight came upon us and we stopped.

Then I thought of a man I used to know who was an old peyote-man. He always spoke to me very kindly. I went over to see him. I thought I would tell him what had happened to me. When I arrived there he was quite delighted. It was about noon and he fed my horses and asked me to eat with him. Then when we were through eating, I told him what had happened to me. He was very glad and told me that I was speaking of a very good thing. Then (finally) he said, "Now I shall tell you what I think is a good thing (for you to do). You know that if an old horse is balky, you can not break him of (this habit); even if you had bought him and tried to break him (of this habit), you would not succeed. If, indeed, you succeeded, it would only be after very hard work. However if you had a young horse, you could train it in any way you wished. So it is in everything. If you marry a woman who has been in the habit of getting married frequently, it would be difficult for her to break herself of a habit she loves. You are not the one she loves. If you marry her you will lead a hard life. If you wish to get married, take your time. There are plenty of good women. Many of them are at (government) schools and have never been married. I think you would do best if you waited for some of these before marrying. They will return in the middle of summer. So, don't think of any of these women you see around here, but wait until then and pray to Earthmaker patiently. That would be the best, I think." I liked what he told me and thanked him. I decided to accept his advice, and I did not look around for women after that. I was to wait about three months and (during that time) I paid strict attention to the peyote ceremony.

On one occasion while at a meeting, I suffered (great pain). My eyes were sore and I was thinking of many things. "Now I do

[181] The metaphor is probably old; its interpretation here, of course, quite new and probably not S. B.'s invention. The peyote people took a number of old Winnebago metaphors, mythical episodes, and mythical characters and gave them specific interpretations.

nothing but pay attention to this ceremony, for it is good." Then I called the leader over to me and said to him, "My elder brother, hereafter only Earthmaker (God) shall I regard as holy. I will make no more offerings of tobacco. I will not use any more tobacco. I will not smoke and I will not chew tobacco. I have no further interest in these.[182] Earthmaker (God) alone do I desire (to serve). I will not take part in the Medicine Dance again. I give myself up (to you). I intend to give myself up to Earthmaker's (God's) cause." Thus I spoke to him. "It is good, younger brother," he said to me. Then he had me stand up and he prayed to Earthmaker (God). He asked Earthmaker (God) to forgive me my sins.

The next morning I was taken home. My eyes were sore and I could not see. They took me back to a house and there they put a solution of the peyote into my eyes and I got well in a week.[183]

One night, when I was asleep, I dreamt that the world had come to an end. Some people Earthmaker (God) took, while some belonged to the bad spirit (devil). I belonged to the bad spirit (the devil). Although I had given myself up (become a peyote-man) I had not as yet been baptized. That was why Earthmaker (God) did not take me. All those who belonged to Earthmaker (God) were marked, but I was not.[184] I felt very bad about it when I woke up, even although I had only dreamt about it.[185] I felt very bad indeed. I wanted them to hurry and have another peyote meeting soon anywhere. I could hardly wait until I reached the place where the next meeting was to take place. I immediately told the leader (what I wanted) and asked him to baptize me and he baptized me in the morning. After that morning I felt better.

Then I went to work and I worked with a railroad work-gang. I was still working when the time for the midsummer celebration approached. I always went to the peyote meeting on Saturday nights.

---

[182] This completes his severance of all the ties that bound him to his former mode of life.

[183] The medicinal virtues ascribed to the old herbs were transferred to the peyote, if indeed we can speak here of a transference and not simply an assimilation of the peyote with the medicinal herbs. It was, as might be expected, one of the earliest claims made for the peyote. Cf. my paper mentioned in note 122.

[184] Used metaphorically to mean "baptized." It is commonly used by the pagan Winnebago to refer to clan identification in spirit-land, i.e., the clan affiliations of the ghosts were considered their marks, quite apart from the fact that of course each clan had its specific facial decorations. This is certainly the source from which S. B. derived the idea.

[185] He claims to have lost his faith in dreams, yet he is intensely desirous of having his defect remedied as soon as possible.

The old man was right in what he had told me. The girl students returned in the summer. Shortly (after they returned) a man, a friend of mine who had gone around with me, asked me if I wanted to get married. "Yes, I do," I answered. Then he said, "Listen, I have been thinking of something. What kind of a woman do you wish to marry?" I told him what I had in mind. Then he said, "Come home with me. I have a younger sister. I want her to marry a good man; I would like to have her marry you," he said. Then I I went home with him. When we got there (and discussed the matter) the girl gave her consent. The parents also consented.

So there I got married and what I expected has taken place and I have lived with her ever since. On one occasion, after she was used to me, she told me this: (Before she had married, she had determined that) if she ever got married, she would not care to marry a very young man. "I wanted a man who ate peyote and who paid attention to the ceremony."[186] Such a man she desired and such a person was I, she said. She loved me, she said, and she was glad that she had married me. That is what she had asked Earthmaker (God) in prayer. "And, indeed, it has happened as I wished," she said. She believed it was the will of Earthmaker (God) that we had done this, she said. She was therefore glad (that she had married me). Together we gave ourselves up (to the peyote) at a peyote meeting. From that time on we have remained members of the peyote (ceremony).

34. I HAVE A STRANGE EXPERIENCE

Many things are said under the influence of the peyote. The members (would) get into a kind of trance and speak of many things. On one occasion they had a peyote-meeting which lasted two nights. I ate a good deal of peyote. The next morning I tried to sleep. I suffered a great deal. I lay down in a very comfortable position. After a while a (nameless) fear arose in me. I could not remain in that place, so I went out into the prairie, but here again I was seized with this fear. Finally I returned to a lodge near the lodge in which the peyote meeting was being held and lay down alone. I feared that I might do something foolish to myself (if I remained there alone), and I hoped that someone would come and talk to me. Then someone did come and talk to me, but I did not feel better, so I thought

---

[186] Exactly what a conservative Winnebago woman might have said in former times.

I would go inside where the meeting was going on. "I am going inside," I said to him. He laughed. "All right, do so," said he. I went in and sat down. It was very hot and I felt as though I were going to die. I was very thirsty but I feared to ask for water. I though that I was certainly going to die. I began to totter over.

I died, and my body was moved by another life.[187] It began to move about; to move about and make signs. It was not I and I could not see it.[188] At last it stood up. The regalia—eagle feathers and gourds—these were holy, they said. They also had a large book there (Bible).[189] These my body took and what is contained in that (book) my body saw. It was a Bible. The regalia were not holy,[190] but they were good ornaments. My body told them that; and that if any person paid attention to Earthmaker's (God's) ceremony, he would be hearkening to what the Bible said; that likewise my body told them. Earthmaker's son (God's Son) said that he was the only Way. This means that one can only get life from the Word.[191] (My) body spoke of many things and it spoke of what was true. Indeed it spoke of many things. It spoke of all the things that were being done (by the pagan Indians) and which were evil. A long time it spoke. At last it stopped. Not I, but my body standing there, had done the talking. Earthmaker (God) had done his own talking.[192] I would be confessing myself a fool if I were to think that I had said all this, it (my body) told me.

After a while I returned to my normal human condition. Some of those there had been frightened, thinking that I had gone crazy. Others had liked it. It was discussed a good deal. They called it the "shaking" state.[193] It was said that the condition in which I was, was not part of Earthmaker's (God's) religion. I was told that whoever ate a lot of peyote would, through the peyote, be taught the teachings of Earthmaker (God). Earthmaker's (God's) ways and man's ways are different.[194] Whoever therefore wished to help this

---

[187] i.e., he was again his soul.

[188] i.e., he was incorporeal.

[189] To the older members of the cult, including the leader Rave, the Bible was merely one of the regalia. To the younger members it was used for interpretations.

[190] This is a new and Christian interpretation. I doubt very much whether Rave would have subscribed to it.

[191] Of biblical origin of course.

[192] As in a previous passage he identifies Earthmaker with his soul.

[193] This condition was regarded as "holy" among the conservative Winnebago likewise.

[194] Of biblical origin and quite foreign to Winnebago thought.

religion must give himself up (to it). If you ate a good deal of this peyote and believed that it could teach you something[195] then it assuredly would do so. That at least is the way in which I understand this matter.

Once we had a meeting at the home of a member who was sick. The sick would always get well when a meeting was held in their home, and that is why we did it.[196] At that meeting I got into the "shaking" condition again. My body told (us) how our religion (peyote) was an affair of Earthmaker's (God's), and even if one knew only a portion of it, one could still see (partake of) Earthmaker's (God's) religion.

Thus it went on talking. "Earthmaker (God), His Son (Christ), and His Holiness (the Holy Ghost),[197] these are the three ways of saying it. Even if you know one (of these three), it means all.[198] Everyone of you has the means of opening (the road) to Earthmaker (God). It is given to you. With that (your belief) you can open (the door to God). You can not open it with knowledge (alone).[199] How many letters are there to the key (the road to God)? Three. What are they?" There were many educated people (there) but none of them said anything. "The first (letter) must be a *K*, so if a person said *K*, that would be the whole of it. But let me look in the book (Bible) and see what that means," said the body. Then it (the body) took the Bible and began to turn the leaves. The body did not know where it was itself, for it was not learned in books.[200] Finally in Matthew, chapter 16, it stopped. There it speaks about it. "Peter did not give himself up" (it says). "For a long time he could not give up his own knowledge. There (in that passage) it says *Key*." That is the work of Earthmaker (God). At

---

[195] It is difficult to determine whether the peyote or the ceremony and its associated beliefs was to teach an individual something. In the former case the notion would be thoroughly Winnebago.

[196] This virtue was also accomplished by a performance of the old pagan rituals and particularly by the Medicine Dance.

[197] This is the peyote translation of the Trinity.

[198] Of Christian origin.

[199] i.e., merely by having read certain things. The inward feeling must accompany the knowledge. This may be in part a criticism of those who could read and quote the Bible glibly and of whose knowledge those members who could not read English were jealous, and whose claims to greater importance they were inclined to resent.

[200] He wished to show that knowledge of English did not give one complete insight into the Bible and its meaning. He probably used Rev. Stucki's translation of the Bible into the language of the Winnebago, of which there were a few copies in Winnebago, Neb.

The theology formulated here is, so far as I know, his own.

least so I understand it. He made use of my body and acted in this manner, in the case of the peyote.

Thus I go about telling (everyone) that this religion is good. Many other people at home said the same thing. Many, likewise, have joined this religion and are getting along nicely.

On one occasion, after I had eaten a good deal of peyote, I learned the following from it; that all I had done in the past, that it had all been evil. This was plainly revealed to me. What I thought was holy, and (by thus thinking) was lost, that I now know was false. (It is false), this giving of (pagan) feasts, of holding (the old) things holy, the Medicine Dance, and all the Indian customs.

35. FINALE

I have written of some of these matters and I have spoken out clearly.[201] I talked about this to the older people but they refused to do it.[202] I thought I would write it down so that those who came after me, would not be deceived.[203] Then my brother had us do this work,[204] (aided by) my older brother[205] and my younger brother.[206]

Before (my conversion) I went about in a pitiable condition, but now I am living happily, and my wife has a fine baby.

This is the work that was assigned to me.[207]

This is the end of it.

---

[201] He was one of my principal informants and wrote down in the Winnebago syllabary a large amount of valuable information.

[202] i.e., he asked other Winnebago to give me certain information, which they refused to do.

[203] This was the reason I gave for asking him to write these matters down.

[204] That is myself.

[205] His older brother, my principal informant, whose knowledge and memory were both remarkable.

[206] My interpreter, Oliver Lamere, who translated practically all the texts I obtained and without whose industry and interest my work would hardly have been successful.

[207] Such was the notion that a number of Winnebago who helped me developed shortly after my coming among them. His brother makes the same statement in my paper mentioned in the Introduction.

PART II. MY FATHER'S TEACHINGS

1. FASTING PRECEPTS[208]

You ought to be of some help to your fellow-men and for that reason (I counsel you) to fast. Our grandfather who stands in our midst sends forth all kinds of (blessings).[209] Try then and obtain one of these. Try to have one of our grandfathers, one of the war chiefs, pity you (bless you).[210] Then some day as you travel along the road (of life) you will know what to do (and encounter) no obstacles. Without any trouble you will then be able to seek the prize you desire. Then the honor will be yours to glory in, for without any exertion (have you obtained it).[211] All the war-power that exists has been donated to our grandfathers who are in control of warfare,[212] and, if, reverently, you thirst yourself to death,[213] then they

---

[208] The Winnebago word means literally "preachings." These preachings were begun when the child was barely old enough to understand them and continued until he or she was about eleven or twelve years of age. Great care was taken not to tire the child; the grandparent or parent watched his pupils and stopped at the first suggestion of fatigue on their part. I believe examples accompanied the sermons but I am not certain. The instructions were given early in the morning.

[209] i.e., Fire, which is regarded as a powerful spirit even today and the worship of which was far more extensive in former times. He was supposed to bestow blessings of the same type as the other spirits—long life, wealth, success on the warpath, etc. In addition, as might be expected, he bestowed upon mortals blessings connected with the home. I know of no recent instance in which he appeared to fasters. At the war-bundle feasts a buckskin is frequently offered to him.
Offerings of tobacco were made to him by throwing them into the fire. Since offerings are made to all the spirits in this manner, a certain amount of confusion has arisen at times as to whether it is the fire or the spirits to whom these belong. My general impression is that what was especially intended for the fire would be announced as such. At the present time, the smoke arising from the fire is regarded as the intermediary between man and the spirits, and this belief has in a way been extended to the fire itself. The former notion is probably extremely old, the latter but one of many indications of the subsidiary role the spirit fire now plays.
The Winnebago explain the frequency of prairie fire as due to the anger of that spirit in not receiving offerings of tobacco any longer.

[210] i.e., any of the spirits who are in control of the powers for victory on the warpath.

[211] i.e., you will have no difficulty in finding out where the enemy is located (the prize) and obtain war-honors. Prize refers not merely to the enemy but also to the war-prizes given to those who kill an enemy and count coup on him. "Without any exertion" means by virtue of the spirits' blessings.

[212] The theological theory is that Earthmaker bestowed (donated) specific powers upon different spirits (our grandfathers). This is referred to later in the text.

[213] i.e., fast, and also have the proper attitude of mind.

will bestow blessings upon you. Now if you do not wear out your feet, if you do not blacken your face (with charcoal), it will be for naught that you inflict (this) suffering upon yourself.[214] These (blessings) are not obtainable without effort. Try to have one of all the spirits created by Earthmaker take pity upon you. Whatever he says will come about. If you do not possess a spirit to strengthen you, and therefore are of no consequence (socially), the people (around you) will show you little respect. They will make fun of you.[215]

It is not good to die in the village. This we tell all those (youths) who are growing up. Do not permit women to journey ahead of you in your village for it is not proper.[216] For these reasons do people encourage one another to fast. Some day you will be traveling on a road filled with obstacles[217] and then you will wish that you had fasted. In order that (when such an event confronts you) you will not find it necessary to blame yourself, (I counsel you) to fast. If you have not obtained any knowledge (been blessed) then some day when (the warriors) return from the warpath and the women are dividing the prizes, your sisters will stand there (empty handed) envying the others.[218] If you obtain blessings from those in control of warfare, then if you are one of the victorious men, your sisters will be very happy; and how proud they will be to receive the prizes, to wear them, and to dance (the victory dance)! Your sisters thereby will also be strengthened.[219] You will be well and happy.

---

[214] i.e., fast repeatedly. The expression "wear out your feet" refers doubtless to the frequent journeys between the lodge proper and the fasting lodge, which were often at some distance from each other.

The complete thought is that attitude of mind is not enough to obtain blessings; you must actually fast and blacken your face. The Winnebago would conceivably have tolerated variations in the attitude of mind required but would never have permitted the omission of blackening one's face. According to a well-known prophecy among them the world will come to an end when the Winnebago fast with "white," i.e., unblackened, faces.

[215] i.e., ridicule you.

[216] i.e., do not die a natural death, and do not die of old age, but die on the warpath. Do not let women die before you. By not "proper" he means here "not proper for a man." In reading all these admonitions it must be remembered that they are not to be taken too literally and that they represent ideals.

[217] This metaphor for the crises of life is frequently used. The notion of life as a road beset with difficulties is common throughout the Woodland and Woodland-Plains region. Among the Winnebago this road is described in exceptional detail in the myth of the journey of the soul to spirit-land.

[218] cf. Introduction.

[219] i.e., they will gain strength in every conceivable sense of the term, but particularly will they gain strength to overcome the crises of life.

Now all this it would be well for you to obtain. However, the older people say that it is difficult to be a leader of men. If you are not such a one and are, instead, merely what we call a warrior,[220] and you do what we call throwing away a (human) life,[221] you will have committed the greatest of all shameful acts. Why, a mourner might hurt you and burn you with embers,[222] and then all your relatives would feel sad on your account.[223] Not with the blessing of one spirit, not even with the blessings of twenty spirits, can you go on the warpath. You should be blessed by all the spirits, those on the earth, those who are pinned through the earth,[224] and those underneath the earth, by all of these; and by all those in the waters, and all those on the sides of the earth, i.e., the winds, all four of them; and by Disease-Giver,[225] the sun; by the moon, the day,[226] the

---

[220] i.e., a common "soldier," not a leader on the warpath. Here it means one who has no authority from the spirits to lead men on a warpath.

[221] i.e., to cause someone to lose his life needlessly. It was expected that everyone who desired to lead a war-party would submit his credentials—specific blessings received in fasting from the spirits—to the chief of the village. If the latter did not consider them sufficient he would forbid the undertaking. He had no authority, however, to prevent it and if the prospective leader chose not to abide by the chief's decision he might proceed, taking with him as many men as cared to go along under the circumstances. If, however, any of these men were killed, the leader of the war-party was held technically guilty of contributing to his death and while it was not regarded as murder it necessitated, I believe, certain payments to the relatives of the deceased, besides bringing shame and ignominy upon the leader and all his kinsmen.

[222] i.e., a relative of the deceased, as he prepares to go into mourning by blackening his face with charcoal (embers), might suddenly in his anger and sorrow actually apply a burning ember to you.

[223] He is very careful to point out that it is the family that is sad through the plight in which the leader finds himself and not the reverse. It must be remembered that he is speaking to a very young child and trying to fire him with enthusiasm for the warrior's life and the old life in general, and he endeavors to avoid placing undue emphasis on any personal suffering that the fictitious warrior may have to endure.

[224] Mythical beings created by Earthmaker in his endeavor to stop the earth from spinning around in space, the condition in which it is represented at the beginning of things. This he succeeds in doing by pinning the earth down by means of four spirits, generally called *Earth-weights* in the myths, placed in the east, north, west, and south respectively. These beings are frequently represented as waterspirits, and are likewise confused with the spirits at the four cardinal points although strictly speaking they have nothing to do with them.

[225] At present a very important deity of the Winnebago, although there are indications that he belongs to a later strata of religious beliefs. He is represented as a being who dispenses life from one side of his body and death from the other. The translation "disease-giver" is only an approximation to a correct rendering of his Winnebago name. He is one of the most important deities connected with war, and blessings from him were quite common.

[226] The Day was a distinct and, formerly, an important deity. In Winnebago the words for day, light, and, in rituals, for life, are identical.

earth;[227] indeed by all those whom Earthmaker put in charge of war blessings and whom he put into the world for that purpose, should you be blessed before you lead a war-party.

If you cast off your dress for many people[228] they will be benefited by your deeds. You will likewise have helped your people. It is good to be honored by all the people and they will then (certainly) like you if you obtain a limb.[229] Far more will they honor you if you obtain two or three or four limbs (count coup four times). Then, whenever people boil an animal, head and body, you will always eat it.[230] However, when you are recounting your war deeds in behalf of departed souls,[231] do not try to add to your honor by claiming more than you actually accomplished. You will thereby merely make the souls (of the departed) stumble in their journey (to spirit-land).[232] If you tell a falsehood there and exaggerate your account, you, in consequence, will die beforehand. Those spirits who are in control of war blessings will hear you. This (the telling of the truth on such an occasion) is sacred. Tell less than you did. The old men claim that it is wiser.[233]

227 It is slightly incorrect to say that all these spirits are in control of war-powers for neither the Moon nor the Earth bestow such blessings. The Moon is almost exclusively a woman's deity. The Earth can be conceived of as "blessing" an individual with the food needed on the warpath, but I know of nothing that the moon could have bestowed on warriors. Incidentally, it might be remarked that the "blessings" for a warpath were supposed to be of the most specific kind and to embrace not merely all those powers essential for killing the enemy and protecting oneself, but also all the food to be consumed by the party, etc. The Disease-giver, the Sun, and the Day are, however, specific war deities. It seems rather strange that the old man does not mention those important and extremely popular war deities, the Thunder-birds.

228 i.e., give away things to the needy. This was done at a number of cere-monies but particularly at the *Herucka* Dance and a special ceremony called the Begging Dance. There were of course, in addition, numerous private occasions when gifts to the poor were made.

229 The regular term for counting coup.

230 You will have the right to eat the choicest parts of the animal, an honor only accorded to great warriors.

231 Do not exaggerate; cf. also note 104.

232 Not merely stumble but stumble as they cross the bridge over the abyss of fire. They will fall in, and, consequently, never reach their destination, thus entailing serious consequences not only upon themselves but also upon their relatives.

The reason so much emphasis is laid upon strict truthfulness in recounting war-exploits is because this is one of the few things about which a Winnebago would be likely to lie, and it is significant to know that the only oaths found are those given, and often demanded, on such occasions. The oath consisted in calling the *Earth* to bear witness to the truth of the statement, and instant death was supposed to be the penalty for perjury.

233 i.e., you stand less danger of unconsciously exaggerating the exploit, but it did not make any difference whether your exaggeration was conscious or uncon-scious, it remained an exaggeration.

On the warpath it is good to die. If you die in war your soul
will not become unconscious.[234] You will then be able to do what you
please with your soul.[235] Your soul will always remain in a happy
condition.[236] If you choose to go back to earth as a human being[237]
and live again you can do so. You can live a second life on earth
or live in the form of those who walk on the light,[238] or in the form
of an animal, if you choose.[239] All these (benefits) will you obtain
if you die in battle.

2. PRECEPTS CONCERNING SOCIAL POSITION AND THE VALUE OF MEDICINES

If you have not obtained (war blessings), fast for your position
in life. If you fast in this way, after you get married you will get
along well. You will then not have to worry about having children
nor about your happiness. If you dream of your home[240] throughout
life you shall be in want of nothing. Fast for the food you are to
receive. If you fast often enough for these things, then some day
when your children ask for food, they will be able to obtain without
difficulty a piece of deer meat, or perhaps even a piece of moose
meat. You (have it within you) to see to it that your children shall
never be hungry.

[234] It is a widespread belief that death is comparable to stumbling and that
consciousness is hardly interrupted. On the basis probably of this notion, rein-
forced by the current belief in metempsychosis, was developed the idea that
especially gifted people, such as priests and warriors, passed directly from one
existence to the other without any loss of consciousness; consciousness meaning
here not the kind ghosts (i.e. the spirits of the departed) have, but a consciousness
identical with that which people possess when living. As to metempsychosis itself
there was no unanimity of opinion, some believing that almost everyone became
incarnated, others insisting that this held for exceptional people only. One of
the principal claims of the Medicine Dance organization was that members
obtained *ipso facto* this boon. The general confusion that exists on this point
now is shown by the fact that, on the one hand it is claimed that a child who
resembles a deceased person is the reincarnation of that person (cf. my paper
mentioned in note 239) while, on the other hand, warriors are supposed to live in
spirit-land in the exact state in which they met death. If they were scalped, so
they would remain, etc.

[235] i.e., you can decide for yourself whether you prefer to remain among the
ghosts leading their beatific life or to become reincarnated.

[236] i.e., you will not suffer either in death or after.

[237] i.e., became reincarnated.

[238] Ritualistic name for birds.

[239] I doubt whether he means that an individual can become permanently
reincarnated in some animal. All the accounts I obtained on this point would
indicate that some individuals passed through a number of animal existences before
they finally decided to resume their human existence again. Cf. such an account
in my sketch, ''The Religion of the North American Indians,'' Jour. Amer.
Folk-Lore, vol. 14, pp. 335–373.

[240] i.e., fast and have the spirits bless you with all that concerns happiness
in a home—a good housewife, children, wealth, and long life.

Now again (let me warn you). Do not abuse your wife. Women are sacred.[241] If you make your wife suffer, you will die in a short time. Our grandmother, Earth, is a woman, and in (abusing your wife) you are abusing her. Most certainly will you be abusing our grandmother if you act thus. Since it is she who takes care of us, by your action you will be practically killing yourself.[242]

When you have your own home, see to it that whoever enters your house obtains something to eat, however little you may have. Such food will be a source of death to you if you withhold it.[243] If you are stingy about giving food someone might kill you on that account; someone might poison you.[244] If you hear of a person traveling through your country[245] and you want to see him, prepare your table and send for him. In this manner you will do good and it is always good to do good, it has been said.

If you see a helpless old person, help him if you have anything at all. If you happen to possess a home, take him there and feed him, for he may suddenly make uncomplimentary remarks about you.[246] You will be strengthened thereby. Or it may be that he happens to carry a box of medicines,[247] which he cherishes very much, under his arms, and offers it to you. If it is a medicine without a stem,[248] keep it to protect your house with. Your home will then never be entered by anything evil, and nothing will enter your house unexpectedly.[249] Such will be your life (if you do what I tell you). Witches will keep away from you.[250] Thus, if you fast, your fellow men will be benefited thereby: Earthmaker created the spirits who

---

[241] I imagine that such an admonition has only become necessary within the last few decades. To apply the epithet *sacred* to women in this general way is unusual. He probably did it to counteract the numerous drunken scenes and wife-beating which a child is likely to witness nowadays.

[242] i.e., she may withhold from you the produce of her body—vegetables, etc., and you will starve to death.

[243] This is a well-known Winnebago proverb.

[244] This, I take it, is an attempt to explain the above proverb.

[245] Visitors seem to have been common in former times and the paying of visits was a favorite custom.

[246] It is considered exceedingly bad form for a guest to admire anything in the house he is visiting. It would imply that he wished to have it and the host would be constrained to give it to him, or, failing that, to make him some other gift. The reverse custom is frequently encountered in rituals but is not common, now at least, in the case mentioned in the text.

[247] Medicines were always kept in a bundle known literally as medicine-depository.

[248] My interpreter explained that this expression refers to those plants that consist entirely of roots, and no part of which appears above ground.

[249] i.e., neither by evil spirits, ghosts, disease, nor by unhappiness in any form. "Unexpectedly" means without giving you some warning and a chance to take measures of precaution.

[250] It is especially at night that these are dreaded.

live above (the earth); those who live on the earth; those who live under the earth; and those who live in the water; all these he created and placed in charge of some (powers). Even the minor (spirits) who move around Earthmaker caused to have rule over some (blessing).[251] In this fashion he created them and (only) afterwards did he create us. For that reason we were not put in control of any (of these blessings). However, Earthmaker did create a weed[252] and put it in our charge, and he told us that none of the spirits he had created would have the power to take this away from us without giving us something in exchange. Thus said Earthmaker. Even he, Earthmaker, would not have the power of taking this from us without giving up something in return. He told us that if we offered him a pipeful of tobacco, if this we poured out[253] for him, he would grant us whatever we asked of him. Now all (the spirits) came to long for this tobacco as intensely as they longed for anything in creation, and for that reason, if with tobacco (in our hands) at any time we make our cry (to the spirits), they will take pity upon us and bestow on us the blessings of which Earthmaker placed them in charge. Indeed so it shall be, for thus Earthmaker created it.[254]

You are to fast. If you are blessed (by the spirits) and breathe upon people[255] you will bring them back to life.[256] You will help your

[251] To this fourfold division of animals two others are frequently added, those who live in the empyrean and those who live below the water. The thunder-birds live in the former and the water-spirits in the latter region.

This "centralization" doctrine, found specifically developed in rituals, belongs clearly to the latest strata of Winnebago religion. Its origin is simple enough. The non-ritualistic myths show clearly that the spirits are essentially *genii loci*, originally presiding over their specific precincts or concerned with their own functions, and contemporaneous with Earthmaker. As the cult of the latter developed most of these spirits were made dependent upon Earthmaker, some of them receiving their powers from him. It is, at bottom, a slight transformation.

[252] i.e., tobacco.

[253] i.e., offered. "Poured out" because it is "poured" from the pipe bowl into the fire.

[254] This represents the rationalization and schematization of an old religious fact, namely, that tobacco is offered to the spirits, and that they bestow blessings upon people. In the gradual process of rationalization the spirits were first thought of as passionately fond of tobacco, and as contracting with mankind to grant blessings to them in return. After that was developed the religious conception that Earthmaker bestowed upon man the exclusive right to tobacco in default of being able to give him anything else, having exhausted all his donations in gifts to the spirits. He told the spirits that they could obtain this delicious tobacco only from human beings, in exchange for the powers he had given them.

[255] i.e., blow your breath upon them and cure them. A Winnebago doctor cured disease by blowing upon the patient and then extracting the object causing the disease. The two actions were quite distinct in nature; the first really constituted the blowing of all the life-giving power obtained by the doctor from the spirits, and the second the actual extracting of the disease. For a description of a medical treatment cf. my paper quoted in note 239.

[256] i.e., restore them to health. Sickness was regarded as a kind of temporary death, or at least as an eclipse of life.

fellow men by doing this. If you will be able to do this (cure the sick) you will be of even more than ordinary help to your fellow men. If you can draw out pain (disease)[257] from inside (the body) you will be of aid to all your fellow men and they will greatly respect you. If you are not working at anything, what you need for sustenance they will give you as long as you live.[258] After your death people will speak about (your deeds) for ever. (In life) they will say, "Really, he has power."

Although you are not able to fast now, do try to obtain this (power i.e., the following power). There are individuals who know (the virtues and powers) of certain plants.[259] It is sad enough that you could not obtain (blessings) during fasting; but at least ask those who possess these plants to take pity on you.[260] If they take pity on you, they will give you one of the good plants that give life (to man)[261] and thus you can use them to encourage you in life.[262] However, one plant will not be enough for you to possess. All (the plants) that are to be found on grandmother's hair,[263] all those that give life, you should try to find out about, until you have a medicine chest (full). Then you will indeed have great reason for being encouraged.

Some of the medicine-men[264] were blessed with life by water-spirits.[265] If you wish to obtain real (powerful) blessings, so that

---

[257] Such is their doctrine of disease. It is never regarded as the absence of the soul, as among many other Indian tribes.

[258] i.e., your patients will, by their fees, support you for life.

[259] i.e., the medicinal qualities of plants. There were two principal medicines among the Winnebago, the Black-earth and the Stench-earth medicines. A very elaborate and extensive feast was connected with the former.

While the actual curing of disease was in the hands of men, the preparation of the herbs was mainly in the hands of women.

[260] i.e., help you. No one was ever "blessed" by a plant during fasting, but tobacco was regularly offered to it and the same phraseology used in addressing it as in exhortations to the spirits. The plant was spoken of as "grandfather" and was "to take pity upon you."

The doctrine referred to here is that man, unaided, can not overcome life's crises. The proper and ideal help is to obtain powers (blessings) from the spirits, but, failing that, to purchase protecting medicines from those who happen to possess them. Blessings from the spirits can not be transferred or purchased because the recipient must even then, theoretically, fast for them.

[261] Here he includes all kinds of plants, medicinal and non-medicinal, that help man to cure disease and enjoy life.

[262] i.e., to spur you on and prevent you from despairing when calamities affect you.

[263] The ritualistic expression used in the Medicine Dance for all the grasses and herbs that grow upon the earth.

[264] i.e., doctors and shamans.

[265] Water-spirits, my translation for the mythical animal spirits known in Winnebago as *Waktcexi*, belong to the older strata of beliefs. They are on the verge of being entirely identified with the evil spirits. This has, as a matter of

you can cure even more people,[266] you will have to fast a long time and sincerely for (these blessings). If four or (perhaps) ten of the powerful spirits bless you, then some day when you have children and anything happens to one of them (i.e., they are sick), you will not have to go and look for a medicine-man (i.e., a doctor) but all you will have to do will be to look into your own medicine chest. Look therein and you will be able to cure your children of whatever ailments they have (with the medicine you find). Not only that, but after a while you will be called (to treat) your fellow-men. Then you can open your medicine chest and you will not be embarrassed for you will know how to treat an individual who is ill[267] and needs medicines since you will possess those that are good for him. You will know where the seat of his troubles exists, and since you will have obtained (these blessings) only after the greatest effort on your part, whatever you say[268] (and do) will be efficacious. If you declare that he will live, then he will live. If you make proper offerings to your medicine, and if you speak of your medicine in the way you are accustomed to do, and if then you ask your medicine to put forth its strength (in your patient's behalf), the medicine will do it for you. If, in truth, you make good offerings of tobacco to your plants, if you give many feasts in their honor, and if you then ask your medicines to put forth their strength, and if, in addition, you talk to them like human beings,[269] then most certainly will these plants do for you (what you ask). You can then accept the offerings (patients

---

fact, taken place to a large extent, for the water-spirits are frequently supposed to mislead fasters with false blessings. Their association with medicinal powers of all kinds was, however, so deeply rooted in the minds of all that it could not be altered; and so even today blessings from water-spirits and, above all, certain peculiar, probably fossilized, bones found in bodies of water and called *water-spirit bones* are regarded as possessing the most extraordinary powers. The water-spirits are the hereditary enemies of the Thunder-birds. They are always pictured as catlike animals with bobbed tails reaching back to the head. Their women are supposed to be the most beautiful in the world.

[266] An efficient and powerful doctor must obtain blessings from a large number of spirits and is supposed to have passed through a number of existences.

[267] Embarrassed means "at a loss." The main advantage, of course, would be the saving of doctor fees which were very high and might be beyond the means of many people. In actual life very few people had doctors in their immediate family and in case of illness doctors were called in. There were never many in any particular village for the requisite blessing was considered the most difficult one to obtain, which I take to mean that the few doctors in a village saw to it that only a few disciples were accepted.

[268] These are among the most difficult blessings to obtain.

[269] i.e., as though it were capable of understanding you as another human being would. The point here is that while the plant is treated as though it were a deity it is after all not a spirit but something that, according to present conceptions at least, is derived from spirits and obtains its virtues from spirits, just as human beings do.

make to you) without any embarrassment and your children will wear these offerings[270] and will gain strength from them. They will be well and happy. So (for all these reasons) be extremely diligent in the care you take of your medicines. Medicines are good for all purposes. That is why they were given to us. We are to use them to cure ourselves (of sickness). Earthmaker gave them to us for that purpose.

If anyone tries to obtain these life-staffs, i.e., the medicines, and inflicts suffering upon himself (in doing so), then our grandmother[271] will certainly learn of it; so whatever you spend (in offerings), she will have cognizance of. She knows all that you have lost in obtaining them (the medicines), and in the long run you will receive back all that you have lost. You gave your offerings for the future.[272] However, even if you obtain more knowledge than this it will be a blessing to you. (It is good) for people to look forward to their future. For all (ailments), for everything, people have medicines. Surely you will not want to be without those things that (all the people) possess.

If, for instance, you should want to obtain the paint-medicine,[273] you would indeed have to make yourself pitiable. If your paint-medicine overcomes your enemy[274] and you keep it in your home, you will never be in want of wealth. This most valued possession people will give you.[275] You will be beloved by all and all this will be caused by (the influence) of the paint-medicine. This paint-medicine is made out of the blood of the water-spirits and is consequently holy. (Some individuals) thirsted themselves to death, and were then blessed by the water-spirits, and thus obtained it. Indeed the water-spirits blessed them with these (gifts); and therefore whatever he (the recipient) tells them (people) will be. Indeed, it will be so. Earthmaker put the water-spirits in charge of these blessings so that the

[270] Apparently wampum or shell necklaces.

[271] "Inflicts suffering" means fasts. As mentioned above one had to fast longer for these and for other blessings. "Our grandmother" is the earth.

[272] The cost of your feasts and the suffering in your fasts will be repaid to you in kind and in degree by the food you will obtain and the happiness you will enjoy. You are really making a good investment for the future.

[273] One of the most powerful of all the magical medicines of the Winnebago. It was made of the "bones" of the water-spirit. That is why it is so difficult to obtain.

[274] A person who had smeared his body with the paint-medicine would be able to attract to himself any enemy he met, so overpowering is its force. It is supposed not only to attract everything to one's person but to paralyze an enemy and utterly deprive him of the power of movement.

[275] i.e., it will attract people so that they will take pleasure in giving you presents. I suppose behind this is also hidden the thought that they are afraid to do otherwise, knowing the power of the medicine.

water-spirits might bestow these upon the people (in fasting). Indeed, so it is.

Some people who wished to find good medicines, discovered the race medicine.[276] Some know (possess) it and it might be well if you tried to learn something about it.

Some have a medicine for courting and some possess one to prevent (married people) from separating; others have one for marriage. Some have a medicine for getting rich. There are others who possess a medicine that will cause people to become crazy. If, for instance, one person has made another one sad at heart, then this latter one can poison him with the medicine (he possesses) and make him crazy. A man can likewise cause a woman, whom he wishes to marry (and who refuses him), to become a harlot by giving her some of this medicine. That is what she would become. This medicine that they know will make her fall in love with all men. Similarly if they wanted a man to be constantly following women, they would give him a medicine that would have that effect. Indeed, any kind of medicine you desire, you can obtain from them (the keepers of these medicines), if you ask them. Some of them have knowledge of plants that put people to sleep, while others know medicines that keep you awake all the time and give you insomnia.[277] Such medicines they are acquainted with. Some know how to overcome the viciousness of dogs who are put to watch over women,[278] by the use of a certain medicine they possess. Some (even) are acquainted with medicines that they use when in a crowd. If they use these when they are in a crowd, people will only notice this one person who is using the medicine and they will consider him a great man.[279] Another medicine possessed by some is for the purpose of preventing people who are traveling from getting tired. They can even cause a dog-fight to take place by the use of a certain medicine. They use medicine

---

[276] i.e., a medicine that will enable you to out-distance anyone in running.

[277] The above-mentioned medicines represent the average Winnebago's medicine chest but do not include those medicines used for specific pursuits such as hunting, fishing, etc. The old man is apparently mentioning them as they occur to his mind, stressing those that obtain for a man the wants most coveted, such as wealth, revenge upon those who do him injury, success in amours, praise, etc.
One of the medicines most feared by women is that used to compel them to yield to a rejected man's passions.

[278] It is quite customary to have dogs guard the young girls when they retire to their menstrual lodges. S. B. mentions this in his autobiography, p. 11.

[279] This gives us a glimpse of the extent of the craving the ordinary Winnebago, and I dare say Indian, has to be singled out from among his fellow-men, and explains in part what seems to us the unusual egotism and conceit evidenced by S. B. throughout every page of his autobiography. It is apparently instilled in boys from their earliest youth.

in connection with everything they do. They would put medicine on the fields they planted. If you protect your fields by having medicine attached to a stick placed in them, no one will pass through them.[280] They (people) would certainly pass through your field if you possessed (no medicines) and they would molest your fields and do as they pleased with them.

People must look out for themselves and try to obtain knowledge of everything so that they can live in comfort (and happiness). Do you also try to learn of all those things you will need. If you find out about these matters, then, as you go along in life, you will not have to buy those things you need,[281] but you will be able to take your own (medicines) and use them. If you act in this manner, and if in addition you fast in the proper way, you will never be caught in life off your guard.[282] If you have a home of your own, your home will appear beautiful and you will never be in want. That is why (I know) you will never afterwards regret these things (that I am telling you). If it so happens that you have to journey in the good (i.e., proper, virtuous) road taken (also) by your fellow men,[283] your actions or fortune in life will never become the butt of other people's jokes (or sarcasm).[284]

If you are not able to obtain anything through fasting, try to have one of the good plants take pity upon you.[285] This I am telling you and if you do not do it, you will certainly suffer thereby. If you do all the things I am telling you, you will benefit by them. If you have not been able to obtain anything in fasting, at least (see to it) that you make use of medicines.[286] If you ever go on the warpath

---

[280] Not because it prevents him but because he would be poisoned if he did. Animals, of course, will also keep away.

[281] Another exhortation to save money or wealth. Protection bought is expensive as well as less efficacious than that which you obtain directly, or, in the case of medicines, possess.

[282] i.e., no unexpected crisis will arise.

[283] i.e., lead the normal virtuous Winnebago life.

[284] cf. note 215.

[285] cf. note 259.

[286] His repeated insistence on this point shows how common is lack of success in fasting. While this may represent the modern demoralized condition of Winnebago culture, it may also reflect a true old cultural fact, namely, that not every one was able to enter into communication with the spirits. It may also represent, in a way, a kind of competition between the power of the medicines and that of the spirits, which, translated into the facts of life, meant a competition between the priests on the one hand and the doctors, shamans, and herbalists, on the other. The greatest rivalry existed between them and they doubtless made all the claims imaginable for their respective powers. Similar competition took place between the priests of the different rituals, notably those of the Medicine Dance and the Sore-Eye Dance.

What the author of these teachings has done here is to make an attempt to give them all their due, and the result is that in each case the particular powers he happens to be discussing are unduly extolled.

you should also use medicine so as not to be hit. Of that medicine you should also have knowledge. There is also a medicine to prevent you from getting′ tired, to enable you to run as long as you wish,[287] (and that) you should also get acquainted with. If it is good, you will never get hungry (while running), and it is this medicine that has accomplished this.

Help yourself as you travel along in life. The earth has many narrow passages scattered over it.[288] If you have something with which to strengthen yourself, then when you get to these narrow passages, you will be able to pass through them safely and your fellow-men will respect you. See to it that people like you. Be on friendly terms with everyone, and then everybody will like you. You will be happy and prosperous.

Never do anything wrong to your children. Whatever your children ask you to do, do it for them. If you act in this manner people will say that you are good-natured.

If anyone in the village loses a friend through death, if you are worth anything (i.e., are wealthy), cover (the expenses) of the (funeral) of the deceased if you can.[289] Help (the mourners) likewise, if you can, in (defraying the expenses of) feeding the departed.[290] If thus you act, you will do well. All the people you have helped will then know you; everyone will know you.[291] For the good you do, all will love you.

It is not good to be a winner (in gambling). You might become rich thereby but that is no life (for anyone to lead).[292] If you are blessed with (luck at) cards, if you are blessed (with the luck of) a gambler, you might indeed win and have plenty (of wealth), but none of the children you have will live. It is said that this (luck at cards) is an affair of the evil spirits.[293]

---

[287] This played a very important part in connection with war exploits, and quite a number of magical devices are known to insure the same characteristics.

[288] The cardinal doctrine of the teachings. Cf. note 208.

[289] The expense of burial falls upon certain relatives and the friend (hitcakaro). It is of course considerable, because in addition to the care of the body, there is the food for the Four Nights' Wake, gifts to the widow, etc.

[290] Food was brought to the deceased's grave for the first four nights after burial, for his spirit was still supposed to be hovering around. His spirit is supposed to reach spirit-land in four days and whether food was brought to the grave after that, I do not know. There was, however, every year a definite day or days set aside for feeding the departed.

[291] i.e., they will know what a fine man you are and you will stand high in their esteem.

[292] The Winnebago, like all Indians, were passionately fond of gambling, but over-indulgence in it was always criticized by the older people.

[293] The first belief, namely, that the children of inveterate gamblers will die, is probably an old one; the second I am inclined to think a new belief.

Now if you do all that I have told you, you will lead a happy and prosperous life. It is for that reason that when the Indians have a child whom they love[294] they preach to him, so that they (the children) would never become acquainted with the things that are not right and never do anything wrong. Then if (in later life) a person did anything wrong, he would do it with a clear knowledge of the consequences of his action.[295] This is all.

3. PRECEPTS CONCERNING MARRIAGE

Now this (the following) they used to say to the men. When you get married do not make an idol of the woman you marry; do not worship her. If you worship a woman she will insist upon greater and greater worship as time goes on.[296] Thus the old people used to say. They always preached against those men who hearken too strongly to the words of women, who are the slaves of women. Sometimes they used to say the following. Now your brother has had many warnings[297] yet it may so happen that he pays no attention to any of them. Perhaps when you are called upon to take part in a war-bundle feast[298] you will refuse to go. It may also be that if you are married, you will listen to the voice of your wife, and you will refuse to go on the warpath.[299] You will appear as if you had been brought up like a girl (and not like a man).[300] All who are men perform the deeds of men; you, on the other hand, will never perform a real man's deed.[301] When you are invited to a war-bundle feast, they will only give you a lean piece of meat.[302] That is what

---

[294] They preach to all children but very likely they tell each child that the boon they are about to confer upon him is one extended only to children whom their parents and grandparents love.

[295] This is a typical and characteristic statement of what a Winnebago father considers to be his duty toward his children. However grieved he may be at his child's disobedience he is absolved from all blame. The child has been warned in time.

[296] Henpecked husbands are by no means uncommon now nor were they in former times.

[297] i.e., he has been told about his attitude by his relatives and in the teachings.

[298] No self-respecting man would ever refuse such an invitation. Nothing more humiliating to the man, and especially to his relatives, could very well be imagined.

[299] Warpath parties were organized in a number of ways. One of the common methods was for a man who felt himself authorized to lead a party, and whose claims had been approved by the chief, to go through the village calling for volunteers. Every real man, especially a young man, was supposed to volunteer and as many were selected as were needed. A henpecked man, even if directly approached, would refuse to join, thus disgracing himself and his kinsmen.

[300] The worst insult that could be hurled against a man.

[301] Said contemptuously.

[302] i.e., the worst part of the meat, given only to people who do not amount to much and have never led a warrior's life.

they will place before you. Why should you run the risk of thus
subjecting yourself to the risk of being made fun of?[303] A real brave
man when he attends a war-bundle feast will be given a deer's head
and you will only receive a (lean) piece of meat in a dish. And that
is all you will get to eat. It will dry up your throat.[304] After a while
you will not even be allowed to go to a feast at all; your wife will
not let you go. If you keep on listening to a woman in this way, all
your relatives will scold you. In time even your sisters will not think
anything of you. They will speak of you and say, "Do not ever go
there." Why, they (your sisters) will not be of any help to you.[305]
Finally, when you have become a real slave (to your wife), if your
wife tells you to hit your own relatives you will do it.[306] It is for
these reasons that it is not good to listen to women. Guard yourself
against it. Do not listen to (women). You will be regarded as different from other people. It is not good.

Remember (also) that women can not be watched. If you try to
watch them and show that you are jealous about them, your female
relatives (in turn) will be jealous of them. Finally, after your
jealousy has developed to its highest pitch, your wife will leave you
and run away (with some one else). You have let her know by your
actions that you worship a woman and one alone, and in addition
you are watching her all the time. As a result she will run away.
On account of this incessant annoyance she will run away. She will
be taken away from you. If you think that a woman (your wife) is
the only one to love, you have humbled yourself,[307] and, in consequence, after a while this woman will be taken away from you. You
have made the woman suffer; you have made her feel unhappy.[308]
Everyone will hear about it. No woman will want to marry you.
You will be known as a very bad man. Now this is all.

---

[303] Appealing to the most sensitive part of a Winnebago's nature.

[304] Meant in a double sense. It is so dry that it will dry up your throat and
you will feel so humiliated and disgraced that your saliva will stop flowing.

[305] Respect for sisters was a fundamental fact among Winnebago. Instances
of it will be found in S. B.'s autobiography.

[306] Nothing more horrible could be conceived of by a Winnebago than a man
striking his relatives at the instigation of his wife. To do so was practically
tantamount to ostracizing yourself.

[307] i.e., humiliated yourself.

[308] Your conduct has made everyone suffer. It is remarkable to see how very
impartial the author, a man, is in this matter. The woman is hardly blamed at
all. The lesson he wishes to point out here is an illustration of the favorite
Winnebago maxim that proportion and sanity are to be observed in everything.

Perhaps you will even act in the following way. When (for instance) people leave (the village) and go on the warpath, then you will join them (knowing) that there it is good to die. Thus you will say because you will feel unhappy about your wife having left you. However, you should not act in that way. You are simply throwing away a life; you cause the leader to throw away a life.[309] If you want to go on the warpath, do not go because your wife has been taken away from you, but if you want to go, go because you feel courageous enough to do it.[310]

On the warpath is the place where you will have fun! However, do not go on the warpath unless you have fasted. You must fast for that particular warpath,[311] for if you do not and you nevertheless try to join such a war-party, then when you are present at a fight, when you are in the very midst of it, a bullet will come your way and kill you. That will be due to the fact that you did not fast. People know this (i.e., to fast) and if, therefore, you depend upon yourself you will certainly do a man's deed.[312] If you have performed any deeds (of valor) recount them to your sisters and your sisters' children and your aunts. Those who are in charge of war-bundles[313] are good to listen to in these matters. Then those whom they counsel will eat an excellent dish,[314] and if they do not succeed in that, then these (the youths admonished) will be able to eat in the middle of the lodge.[315] Of such things it was that they spoke and I want you

---

[309] You are throwing your life away, because, in the first case, you have had no authority from the spirits to go on the warpath, and in the second your attitude of mind is not the proper one, for, as pointed out before, success depends upon the proper external and internal conditions.

[310] This is the ethical corollary he draws from the above-mentioned instance.

[311] While during the puberty fast the blessings received might be taken to hold for life, as a matter of fact they can be said to have been in reality merely a necessary preliminary to the blessings required for every specific undertaking. The one permanent possession obtained during the puberty fast was the guardian spirit.

The members of one clan, the Hawk or warrior clan, claimed that they had the right to go on the warpath without fasting for powers beforehand, but their claims were ridiculed by the other clans and it seems that as a matter of fact they, like the others, did fast on such occasions. Such discrepancies between claims advanced and the actual facts were quite common and exemplify again the tendency for an organization, be it social as in this case, or religious, to insist that certain privileges or powers are connected with membership.

[312] Killed an enemy, counted coup, stolen a horse.

[313] i.e., the custodians of the war-bundles. The author of these precepts was the owner and custodian of one of the most famous war-bundles, that of the Thunder-bird clan.

[314] A metaphorical expression for "will eat the choice part of the deer served to distinguished warriors at the war-bundle feast."

[315] I think he is referring to the honor so dramatically described by S. B. in his autobiography (p. 15) where a noted warrior eats out of the same plate with you and transfers some of his powers to you. The idea is the same as exhorting those who were unable to obtain a blessing in their fasts at least to purchase protecting medicines.

to do the things about which they are speaking. That is the advice I give you; that is what (I wish) to say to you. Whatever was to be done (in life) that they spoke about to one another clearly.

I myself never asked for these things, but my father did. He asked for them, he told me. And your grandfather did the same; he asked for the information relating to the manner in which human beings are to behave. Never (in life) when you are older should you allow yourself to get in the predicament of not knowing what is the right thing to do, if you are asked. Ask for this instruction, my children, for it is not a matter of fact affair.[316] You must learn these teachings.

4. PRECEPTS TAUGHT A WOMAN

Now thus they (the old people) spoke to a woman.

Women, as you travel along the path of life, listen to your parents. Do not let your mother work. Attend to the wants of your father. All the work in the house belongs to you. Do not shirk it. Chop wood, pack it; look after the vegetable (gardens), gather them and cook them. When you move back to the village in the spring of the year to live there, plant your fields immediately. Never get lazy. Earthmaker created you (to do these things).[317]

When you get your menses, do not ask those in the house[318] to give you any food. Fast, and do not eat until you get back to the house.[319] If you act in this manner, you will be fasting for your

---

[316] i.e., it is not anything that you can think out in a minute or two, it is something that must be learnt and thoroughly known.

[317] This gives us a fairly complete idea of what were considered the duties of a woman from a man's viewpoint. It is interesting to see how the teacher finds it necessary to give the child a reason for his admonitions—Earthmaker has so willed it.

[318] A woman retires to a special lodge built for her near her parents' or grandparents' lodge, when she has her menstrual flow, and is not supposed to have any intercourse with her family until her period is over and she has bathed. Her food is brought to her. She is not allowed to touch it with her hands, but must use sticks to convey it to her mouth. There are a number of other taboos she must observe. For instance, she is not allowed to look at the sun directly, but she may look at it through smoked glass.

There is one custom mentioned frequently by S. B. in his autobiography that seems almost incredible and that I was at first inclined to believe of very recent origin, namely, that women were courted while staying in their menstrual lodges. The most satisfactory explanation that I can give is that they stayed in these lodges after their menstrual flow had ceased and that these lodges became, in a manner, small clubhouses for women; for frequently a number of young unmarried women retired together.

[319] I believe he means the regular food, for the food given them on these occasions was very simple. I do not believe that women were supposed to fast in the same sense that men were, and the comparison of the puberty fasts of boys with the first menstrual lodge of girls is only partly true. The whole matter is rendered doubtful and confusing because practically all our information on this point comes from men.

seat.[320] Your seat you can only keep by fasting. Then when you marry, even if the man has been a good-for-nothing before, your husband will become a good hunter. And this will be on your account. You will not fail in anything. You will be happy (and contented). If, on the contrary, you do not do as I tell you, then when you marry you will weaken him. You will be to blame for this. After a while your husband will become sickly.[321]

It is not good to use medicine. If you marry a man and place medicine on his head, you will weaken him and he will not amount to anything. It may happen that you do not want your husband to leave you, and that you reflect about the matter and then use some medicine; that you place medicine upon your husband's head.[322] It is not good. You will be ruining a man. It will be equivalent to killing him. Do not do it. It is forbidden. If you marry a man and want to live with him permanently, work for him in order to hold him. If you marry a man, listen to what he says. If you do your work properly and the man likes you, he will never leave you. By working (for him) you must make your husband love you.[323] It is not proper to use medicine. Before you are fairly mature in years, do not use any medicine. You will merely weaken yourself and your life will be of no importance (i.e., weak). Perhaps you will cause the medicine to work on yourself[324] and you will become foolish (demented).

---

[320] i.e., your position in life; a metaphor used in the rituals where the "seats" were assigned according to the honor in which the host held certain individuals. Thus, a "good seat" is an honorable position in life. In popular language the same thing is expressed by a "good dish" or "good plate." "To have your dish upset" means to have misfortune, etc.

[321] As in the instructions to the boys, the instructor tried to attribute success to their willingness to follow his admonitions and failure to their disobedience, so here he tries to show that success in the most important affairs of a woman's life will depend upon her adherence to what he is telling her. Even a worthless man, a poor hunter for example, will become an honorable man and a good hunter if he possesses a virtuous, custom-abiding wife. And vice versa a women who refuses to fast for "her seat" will cause her husband (presumably a virtuous husband) to become ill. Nothing of the kind, we have just seen, was told the young boys.

[322] He is referring to the temptation that young wives might have to do this. An instance of such an attempt is mentioned by S. B. in his autobiography. As S. B.'s actions indicate, men were extremely afraid of it.

[323] This is, of course, all from the man's viewpoint. The woman's is likely to be considerably different in this as it is on other questions. The main point, however, the exhortation to work properly, would be acquiesced in by every woman.

[324] If the first reason, namely that it would cause her prospective husband to become ill, does not seem sufficiently strong, as conceivably it might not, considering the fact that the girl is extremely young, and since she is, in addition, represented as resorting to it for what might seem a justifiable purpose, namely the retention of her husband's affections, the instructor impresses upon her the danger of the medicine applied to her husband working upon herself and causing her to become

Do not use medicine when you are married. Marry only one person at a time. Do not marry several people. Be good and virtuous in your married life. If you do not listen to what I say and are bad, all men will make fun of you. Whatever they wish they will tell you.[325] They will joke familiarly with you about everything and everybody. As a matter of fast, everybody who wants to will tease you. Therefore, if you do not listen to me, you will injure yourself.[326]

Thus, it is said, the old people spoke to one another, and thus they handed down (these precepts, from one generation to another). They warned (the young) people against those things that it was not right to do. They also said that when a girl grows up they should preach to her, and that is why I am telling you these things.

As you grow older, when you get to be a young woman, the men will court you. Now never hit a man.[327] It is forbidden. If you dislike a man very much, tell him gently to go away. If you do not act in this way and instead strike him, remember that frequently men possess certain (injurious) medicines, and that even if the particular person whom you have made sad at heart does not possess this kind of medicine, he knows from whom to get it. They will use this medicine on you, and as nice and chaste as you have been, you will change and run away with someone. You will be of no consequence. They will do this to make you wicked. They will make you do whatever they wish. This is what they (the old people) are afraid of and why they warn you about these things. Hope with all your heart that you do not fall into such a predicament. I really mean what I say.

Do not be haughty to your husband. Do whatever he says. Kindness will be returned and he will treat you in the same way that you treat him.

---

demented. Such may be a Winnebago belief, but the danger a woman ran, in Winnebago eyes, lay not in this but in the probability of her husband in return applying some magical medicines to her. The instructor is clearly trying to frighten the young woman. He is also substituting some dire consequence she can understand for another which is certainly a good old Winnebago admonition to girls but possibly devoid just then of concrete significance.

[325] i.e., they will have no respect for you such as is shown a man's wife, and will treat you as if they were on joking-relationship terms with you. Just as it was regarded as good form to joke with those to whom you stood in this relation, so it was considered exceedingly unbecoming and improper to do it unjustifiably. If a man made an improper remark to a woman, her answer always was, ''On what joking-relationship terms am I with you?'' equivalent to our ''How dare you, sir!''

[326] Subject yourself to the risks of being insulted and of feeling miserable.

[327] Young girls, I was given to understand, were very direct in their expression of dislike, and that women were capable of striking men when sufficiently aroused is demonstrated by the very amusing episode mentioned by S. B. in his autobiography, (p. 40).

If you have a child (and it is naughty), do not strike it. In olden times if a child was naughty the parents did not strike it, but made the child fast. When he is quite hungry he will reflect upon his disobedience.[328] If you hit him you will merely put more naughtiness into him.[329] It is also said that women (mothers, etc.) should not lecture the children, that they merely make the children bad by admonishing them. Thus it would be, those who admonish us declare. Likewise, if your husband says (scolds) anything to the children, do not take their part for then they will become very bad indeed. That is why you should not take their part. If a stranger makes your children cry, do not speak to the stranger in your children's presence and take their part. If you wish to take the children's part, prevent such a thing from happening and keep your children home, and there, at home, take good care of them and think of the best means of letting your children get to know you. When you are bringing up children, do not imagine that you are taking their part if you just speak about loving them. Let them see it for themselves. Let them see (what love is) by seeing you give things away to the poor. Then they will see your good deeds and then they will know whether you have been telling the truth or not.[330]

Do not show your love for other children so that people notice it. Love them but let your love for them be different from your love (for your own). If you are wicked you will love other people's children more than your own. The children of other people are different from your own and if they were to be taken to some other place, they would become estranged. Thus they would not belong to you any longer. You can, on the contrary, always depend upon your own children because they are of your own body. Love them, therefore. This is the way our ancestors lived.[331]

---

[328] In old accounts of Indians there is frequent mention of these precepts in bringing up children and it is claimed that the children, in consequence, were ungovernable. There is no indication of this now and the older authors were probably referring to what they deemed wildness, etc. Winnebago children are remarkably well-behaved, respectful, and obedient, and this is all attained without whipping or unduly scolding them.

[329] i.e., you will make them stubborn and they will probably persist in their acts of disobedience.

[330] Here we have a complete system of education the main characteristics of which are: teaching conduct by example, preventing occurrences that a child should not witness, and the recognition that the child has a mentality of its own, that it may be able to distinguish words from deeds and that it may even be capable of knowing whether its parents are living up to their professions.

[331] They mean not merely their own children by blood but also their adopted children. Between the two very little difference was made.

If you, a woman, do not have any real interest in your husband's welfare and affairs, then you will be to him like any other woman. People will ridicule you. If, on the other hand, you pay more attention to your husband than to your parents, if you listen to him more than to them, that will be equivalent to deserting them for good.[332] Let your husband keep your parents and take good care of them, for they depend upon him. Your parents saw to it that you married him and they expect you to make some return for this, as well as for the fact that they raised you.[333]

The old people also said that you were not to hurt the feelings of your relatives. If you hurt their feelings you will make your brothers-in-law feel ashamed on account of the evil things you say about them.[334]

Never desire any other man than your husband. He should be enough. Have only one husband. Do not let anyone have the right to call you a prostitute.

The old people also said: "Never hit your relatives. If you happen to be on bad terms with one of your relatives, he may die and people will say, 'That person used to quarrel with the deceased when he was alive.' They might even claim that you were pleased at his death, and that you (want to) dance (for joy). Then indeed will you be sore at heart, and you will think, 'What can I best do (to make amends)?' Even if you have a medicine dance performed for the deceased,[335] if you bury him with honor,[336] even then people will say, 'She used to be partial and jealous. Now when he is dead, she loves him. She ought not to do these things. She is merely wasting a lot of money. She need not have spent so much.'[337] Thus they

---

[332] The family ties were extremely strong, of course, and as the woman left both family and clan when she married, she was always in danger of becoming estranged from her own people.

[333] A man generally went to live with his wife's parents for the first year after marriage and worked for them. He then usually built a lodge for himself. That he was expected to take care of his wife's parents I had never heard before. I do not believe, therefore, that the instructor is referring to an actual custom; he is simply impressing upon his daughter her duty toward them. This seems borne out by the reasons he gives.

[334] Why brothers-in-law are specially selected I do not know. He seems to be referring to relatives by marriage.

[335] cf. description in S. B.'s autobiography.

[336] i.e. not omitting any of the customs and having an elaborate Four Nights' Wake to which many warriors are invited, because the more war exploits that are related the greater will be the number of enemy souls that will be placed at your deceased relative's disposal.

[337] Here again we have the doctrine of proper observances and proper attitude; one without the other is of no avail.

will speak about you. Indeed, then your heart will ache. Perhaps you will even get very angry when they say these things about you! It is (to prevent this) that the older people say, 'Love one another!' If you have always loved (a person) then when he dies you will have a right to feel sorrow.[338] People will feel that (your grief) is honest. All your relatives will love you,' and not only they, but everyone else as well. If you behave like a (true) woman everyone will love you, and then if it happens that you meet with some crisis in life, all the people will turn their hearts to you in your trouble. That is all I wish to say about this matter.

It will be good if you conduct yourself in the way I have just told you. That is what I wish you to do. For instance in your home, where you have been raised, doubtless they know all about domestic work, about hunting,[339] and the work around a camp. If you too learn these matters then some day when you visit your husband's relatives, you will not find yourself in an embarrassing position from which you can not extricate yourself. When you are visiting your husband's people do not walk around in a haughty manner. Do not act as if you were far above them. Try to get them to like you. If they like you, you will be put in charge of the camp in which you are living. Indeed if you are good-natured you will be put in charge of the home of the people with whom you are camping.[340] If on some future occasion you act in this way, then the parents of your husband will say to him, 'Our daughter-in-law treats us well. Whatever there is in this camp, she may be in charge of. She has (also) raised children for you.' This is all (I wish to say on this matter).''

5. HOW KNOWLEDGE IS OBTAINED FROM THE OLD MEN[341]

In the olden times if a man loved a child very much he would teach him these things. However, you would not be taught these things without paying. Under all circumstances you must fast all day before you are taught.

---

[338] Sorrow is not a feeling that belongs to you as an inalienable right, i.e., true sorrow. Sorrow is something which you feel when you have lost a person you have loved and when your fellow-men have been the witnesses of your love and your acts of love.

[339] A woman was supposed to take care of the animal after its body had been placed in front of the lodge. That is apparently what is referred to here, for she had nothing to do with the actual hunting.

[340] There are a number of Winnebago proverbs bearing on these points. For instance, ''Never think a home is yours unless you make one yourself''; ''If you are living with people and have put them in charge of your household, do not, nevertheless, act as though the home were yours.''

[341] What follows is a description that might apply to the obtaining of any kind of knowledge.

When a man has come to consciousness,[342] i.e., when he is grown up, the old people will demand a certain payment (for what they are about to teach you). When they ask you about it (the payment, i.e., the fasting) you must tell them truthfully whether you have begun to fast. For then those who have been preaching to you will stop. Otherwise they would find themselves preaching to men[343] and not boys.

Then (the youth) went up to the old man and said, "Grandfather, my father sent me here to ask you something." Thus he spoke. "I would like to know how to lead an upright life. Give me your blessing,[344] and if you can tell me anything, please do it," he said. The old man was very grateful for these words. "You speak the truth," he said. Now the young man who was asking these favors of the old man had taken good care of his body. He had led a blameless life and he had no scar of any kind.[345] The old man was about to eat, so the young man brought all sorts of presents into the lodge. He gave him also a fine saddle-horse. Then the young man asked what kind of a life (his ancestors) had led; all such things he inquired about.

Then he asked what one does when a child is to be given a name. On such an occasion you are to say what I told (before). As I have told you, it may happen if someone knows you that they will put a child before you to be named. If then you are called upon to say anything you will not have to behave like a deaf and dumb man. If you are asked, you will know what to say.[346] You will do it well. A small child will be offering you the means to show your power[347] and you will smoke his tobacco and you will be giving a feast (in his honor). There (at the feast) give the child (the right to use) some dog-name that you cherish greatly.[348] Tell him also in great detail what the dog-name means. Do not open your mouth too widely[349]

---

[342] This expression is also used by S. B. in his autobiography (p. 3) to indicate his first recollections.

[343] They have passed from the period of childhood (nɪnkdjɪck') to that of youth (hodja'na).

[344] i.e., the benefit of some of the blessings you have obtained. It has no Christian connotation whatsoever.

[345] i.e., he had done nothing wrong, or against the teachings of the tribe.

[346] i.e., you will possess the knowledge necessary.

[347] i.e., you will be asked to give some child a name.

[348] In addition to the child's name, dog-names were presented to a person at a naming feast.

[349] i.e., open your mouth as though you were actually going to say something important and then say nothing of consequence.

but say something. If you are to give him a name for a male dog, give him the name *Yellow-tree,* which refers to what a tree looks like after it has been struck by thunder-birds.[350] Just as leaves wither, so do trees (wither) when the thunder-birds strike them. Soon after that they commence to rot; they get discolored. That is what the name of this dog means, it is said.

When a name is given to a female child, the members of the clan[351] gather together. Should you be placed among them (as the name-giver), after you have finished making your speeches, then you must give her (the child) a name for a female dog. Give her the name *Stays-at-her-own-place.* Then if this child ever possesses a female dog, she will have a name for it. The warrior, bear, wolf, and all the other clans, have specific things to say (at such a feast) and they also have specific dog-names. This is the end.

---

[350] Personal names are now either explained in this manner or as having refer-ence to the legendary creation of the tribe at Green Bay, Wisconsin. Cf. my paper ''The Social Organization of the Winnebago Indians,'' Bull. 10, Anthro-pological series of the publications of the Geological Survey of Canada.

[351] Names are generally given by members of your clan unless you wish to honor your friend-clan and ask a member of that clan to bestow a name, or unless you are not wealthy enough to pay for the name. In the latter case a number of things may happen. Generally the mother's clan will give the child a name taken from its clan.